friendly and rich with imagery that serve to activate and cultivate the imaginal sense ... Dr. Kaehr's clear instructions in how to let go and forgive in order to find the lesson in life's sometimes difficult teachings will be a balm to those in need of deeper understanding of life's challenges."

—Neale Lundgren, PhD, author of *Meditations for the Soul*

JOURNEYS
THROUGH
the
AKASHIC
RECORDS

ABOUT THE AUTHOR

For two decades, **Shelley A. Kaehr, PhD** (Dallas, TX) has worked with thousands of people around the world helping them achieve greater peace and happiness in their lives. A world-renowned past-life regressionist, Dr. Shelley's method of combining energy work with hypnosis has been endorsed by numerous leaders in the field of consciousness, including near-death experience pioneer Dr. Raymond Moody and Dr. Brian Weiss. Dr. Shelley has been prominently featured in the media, including *Coast to Coast AM* and William Shatner's *Weird or What*. She received her PhD in Parapsychic Science from the American Institute of Holistic Theology in 2001.

Connect with Dr. Shelley Kaehr via her website:
https://pastlifelady.com
Facebook Fan Page: Past Life Lady
Instagram: shelleykaehr
YouTube: Past Life Lady
Twitter: @ShelleyKaehr

JOURNEYS THROUGH the AKASHIC RECORDS

Accessing Other Realms of Consciousness for Healing and Transformation

SHELLEY A. KAEHR PhD

LLEWELLYN PUBLICATIONS
Woodbury, Minnesota

First Edition
First Printing, 2022

Book design by Colleen McLaren
Cover design by Shannon McKuhen
Editing by Laura Kurtz

Llewellyn Publications is a registered trademark of Llewellyn Worldwide Ltd.

Library of Congress Cataloging-in-Publication Data (Pending)
ISBN: 978-0-7387-6944-8

Llewellyn Worldwide Ltd. does not participate in, endorse, or have any authority or responsibility concerning private business transactions between our authors and the public.
    All mail addressed to the author is forwarded but the publisher cannot, unless specifically instructed by the author, give out an address or phone number.
    Any internet references contained in this work are current at publication time, but the publisher cannot guarantee that a specific location will continue to be maintained. Please refer to the publisher's website for links to authors' websites and other sources.

Llewellyn Publications
A Division of Llewellyn Worldwide Ltd.
2143 Wooddale Drive
Woodbury, MN 55125-2989
www.llewellyn.com

Printed in the United States of America

ALSO BY SHELLEY A. KAEHR, PHD

*Beyond Reality: Evidence of
Parallel Universes* (Out of This World, 2014)

*Blast from the Past: Healing Spontaneous
Past Life Memories* (Llewellyn, 2021)

*Familiar Places: Reflections on Past Lives
Around the World* (Out of This World, 2016)

*Heal Your Ancestors to Heal Your Life: The Transformative
Power of Genealogical Regression* (Llewellyn, 2021)

Lifestream: Journey into Past & Future Lives
(Shelley Kaehr/Out of This World, 2020)

*Meet Your Karma: The Healing Power
of Past Life Memories* (Llewellyn, 2021)

Past Lives with Gems & Stones (Self-published, 2014)

*Past Lives with Pets: Discover Your Timeless Connection
to Your Beloved Companions* (Llewellyn, 2020)

*Reincarnation Recollections: Geographically Induced
Past Life Memories* (Out of This World, 2016)

*Supretrovie: Externally Induced
Past Life Memories* (Out of This World, 2016)

DISCLAIMER

This book is not intended as a substitute for consultation with a licensed medical or mental health professional. The reader should regularly consult a physician or mental health professional in matters relating to his/her health and particularly with respect to any symptoms that may require diagnosis or medical attention. This book provides content related to educational, medical, and psychological topics. As such, use of this book implies your acceptance of this disclaimer.

Names and identifying details have been changed to protect the privacy of individuals.

ACKNOWLEDGMENTS

To my amazing and supportive editor and friend Angela Wix, I thank you. This book would not exist without you. To my students who requested a class on the records that evolved into this book and to the many souls I've had the privilege of working with over the years, I'm thankful for your support and encouragement. Special thanks to Janine MacVey, Damaris Hopewell, Lynn Wiederhold, Maria Wirges, Theresa Hallinan, Bob Paddock, Maya Martillini, and Lori Mitchel.

I also give my sincere thanks and extreme appreciation to the entire Llewellyn team, who are absolutely phenomenal! There are literally no words to express how very grateful I am for your support of all my ideas and for giving me the space and time to express them! Heartfelt thanks to Bill Krause, Terry Lohmann, Kat Sanborn, Anna Levine, Lauryn Heineman, Andy Belmas, Shannon McKuhen, Sami Sherratt, Jake-Ryan Kent, Alisha Bjorklund, Lynne Menturweck, Patti Frazee, Kevin Brown, Donna Burch-Brown, Leah Madsen, Sammy Penn, Laura Kurtz, and the rest of the Llewellyn team.

I am extremely grateful also to the phenomenal Dr. Linda Howe, founder of the Center for Akashic Studies, a real pioneer and groundbreaker in the field of Akashic Records. Dr. Howe was the first person to ever earn a Doctorate in Spiritual Studies from Emerson Theological Institute with her emphasis in Akashic Studies. Her wonderful books and classes have helped many understand the nature of the Akashic Records, and I am proud to call her my friend. Special love and gratitude to my lifelong friends Dr. Raymond Moody and George Noory. I extend my love and appreciation to my family and friends including Jim Merideth, Pat Moon, and Paula Wagner. And above all, I owe a debt of gratitude to my readers. This book is for you!

CONTENTS

EXERCISES

INTRODUCTION

Welcome to *Journeys through the Akashic Records*. I'm so excited to explore the Akashic Records with you! Since I first learned about reincarnation in childhood, I believed that we lived in prior lifetimes, and my fascination with that philosophy led me to pursue a career as a regressionist. Humans are complex. No two people are exactly alike. Regardless of what popular culture may want us to believe, there's no one-size-fits-all remedy to the challenges we face as individuals. Each soul comes to their current incarnation with a specific set of ideals and lessons to learn, memories of all the lifetimes they've lived before, people they're meant to meet, old business to finish up, and specific filters through which they process the world. I discovered during private sessions that most of the time, my clients needed far more than a mere past-life regression in order to heal. *Journeys Through the Akashic Records* represents the culmination of my work as a past-life regression practitioner that I am making available to the public for the first time. Within these pages, I will reveal more of the processes I've used to help my clients achieve greater peace.

The Akashic Records consist of all thoughts, deeds, and actions that have ever been created in the past, present, or future. I've been accessing the Akashic Records quite frequently ever since my near death experience back in 2000. I went into the light and returned to my body with expanded knowledge of concepts completely out of the realm of my current life experience. Healing vibrations poured through my hands, and I had a keen awareness of the vast web of interconnected consciousness that I had no idea what to call at the time. I now understand I tapped into the Akashic Records, the unlimited storehouse of energy and information.

After that experience, several wacky things started happening. For no apparent reason, when people talked to me, my mind wandered into a different dimension of reality where I witnessed people's firsthand experiences as if sitting atop their shoulders. Even the most mundane things like trips to the grocery store, the mailbox … you name it, I saw it. I could also access information about people—who they were in their prior lifetimes, their soul purposes, and life lessons—even though I made no conscious attempt to do so. I felt confused, to say the very least. Over time, this strange ability became quite distracting, as you can imagine. I took energy healing classes and simultaneously learned techniques to block my super sensitivity so I could function properly in the real world.

At the same time, I realized my experience could be used to help other people. Although I could easily tell people who they were in a past life, I chose to focus on guided imagery instead because of my steadfast belief that self-discovery is far more beneficial in the long run than receiving psychic readings. I combined the modalities of past-life regression with energy healing and intuitive reading and guided clients through a multi-faceted procedure to help them access their past lives and future memories. Clients projected their consciousness into an unrealized current life future to a place where they felt happy, healthy, and knew beyond a shadow of a doubt that no matter what troubles they faced, in the end, those issues would be resolved. The sessions evolved over time to include journeys into a vast network of multidimensional space where my clients experienced meaningful visionary encounters with whatever people or issues they needed to face in order to achieve peace. I discovered such places could be accessed through multidimensional doorways that led into a space I called the *Mindstream.*

Mindstream is a Buddhist term used to describe the interconnected nature of all beings and of reality itself.[1] Strangely, I began calling this inner-dimensional space the Mindstream years before I ever consciously discovered the connections to Buddhism. I can only assume this has to do with my own past-life memories, as I do believe I lived in different parts of Asia in ancient times, although my conscious recollection of those prior incarnations is often quite vague. Mindstream in Buddhism emphasizes the importance of your eternal mind. Consciousness survives bodily death, and the soul simultaneously lives on in other lifetimes and realities. This web of consciousness is filled with information widely known as the Akashic Records. The Mindstream is the terrain, and the Akashic Records are the pieces of wisdom found within that territory that exists eternally within time and space. By knowing which doorways to walk through within the Mindstream, seekers can experience other realms of existence that are not accessible through the typical five senses alone.

My clients' personal revelations after traveling into the Mindstream and accessing their own Akashic Records proved far more meaningful than anything I could have ever told them outright. For this reason, I'm sharing the many guided imagery journeys I've developed over the years with you in this book so you can benefit from these methods yourself without having to spend a ton

---

1. Tenzin Gyatso, the Fourteenth Dalai Lama and Thubten Chodron, *Approaching the Buddhist Path* (Somerville, MA: Wisdom Publications, 2017), 37.

of money to do so. I will show you how to successfully enter the Mindstream and gain access to the Akashic Records of all things past, present, and future that relate to your personalized journey as a soul traveling through time; and you'll discover the information that is meant for you to receive during your current lifetime.

Although I first accessed the Akashic Records through a kind of divine intervention, I wholeheartedly believe anyone with the proper desire, technique, and intention can enter the Mindstream and access the inexhaustible wellspring of information available within the Akashic Records. This book will enable you to visit your own personal distinctive mystical spaces and find custom-made answers to life's most perplexing questions.

You can resolve issues that you've been wondering about for years, if not most of your life by exploring the multidimensional doorways within the Mindstream and finding the specific Akashic Records that will shed meaningful light on your personal understanding and healing. You will acquire detailed information regarding your soul's mission, your unique purpose, and what you're meant to do during your current life experience. You'll also learn how to keep your own counsel, rather than relying on an outside source to give you the answers you need to emerge victorious in life. Personal experiences of your own higher self and the wisdom you already possess can help you move toward a state of confident self-reliance, resilience, and mastery you can use to overcome the many challenges of modern society. You have the power within you to find answers to the questions you face in your life. I'm so excited to take this journey with you! I pray this book has found you at just the right moment to make a profound impact on you for years to come.

HISTORICAL REFERENCES TO THE AKASHIC RECORDS

Akasha means "sky," "space," or "ether" in Sanskrit.[2] As the name suggests, the Akashic Records are often defined as a cosmic storehouse comprised of all things in the universe that have ever or will ever happen. After working in the field of past-life regression and through my research into the past-life accounts of my clients, I've become a huge fan of world history. Studying notable historical figures and references to the Akashic Records is a great starting point to understand why people place such value in them. One could argue that any gifted artist, writer, musician, savant-leveled genius or futurist relays their gifts to humanity by tapping into the inexhaustible knowledge contained within the Akashic Records. Here are a very few of the most notable and fascinating examples.

NOSTRADAMUS (1503–1566)

Famed French born prophet Michel de Nostradame not only became a gifted seer and astrologer but initially followed in his family's footsteps by working as a medical doctor during the height

---

2. A. Pablo Ianonne, *Dictionary of World Philosophy* (Routledge, NY: Taylor & Francis, 2001), 243.

of the Black Death. Nostradamus successfully applied unconventional medical techniques to save several patients. Sadly and ironically, his own wife and children succumbed to the plague in 1534, sending Nostradamus into his more esoteric work of prophecy. He crafted his future predictions in the form of poetic quatrains, claiming that his prognostications arose from combining his visions and astronomical calculations. After entering a hypnotic trance state induced by staring into flames, Nostradamus used herbs and a brass tripod to shift his frequency. The first quatrain of "Century One of the Prophecies" described his method:

> *Sitting alone at night in secret study;*
> *it is placed on the brass tripod.*
> *A slight flame comes out of the emptiness and*
> *makes successful that which should not be believed in vain.*[3]

These sittings proved miraculous in that Nostradamus lived during threat of the Inquisition and somehow eluded authorities and survived. His numerous quatrains containing stunningly detailed warnings of future events also contained vague nonsense that allows modern seekers to continue to apply new meanings to his predictions. Regardless of whether you believe in Nostradamus's talent or not, the source of his information likely originated in the Akashic Records.

THEOSOPHICAL SOCIETY AND THE AKASHIC RECORDS

One of the reasons the Akashic Records are so popular in our culture today is thanks to the groundbreaking research and writings

---

3. Nostradamus, *The Complete Prophecies of Nostradamus* (Radford, VA: Wilder Publications, 2007).

of members of the Theosophical Society. Here are a few of the key members who spoke of the Akashic realm.

- *Madame Helena Blavatsky* (1831–1891): I'm constantly surprised by the number of students I meet who have never heard of the famed Madame Blavatsky, co-founder of the Theosophical Society. I've personally been drawn to her writings and teachings for years to the point that I feel as though I had been a follower of her work in a prior lifetime. Born in what is now modern-day Ukraine, Blavatsky reported having mystical experiences as a child, including encounters with Tibetan Mahatmas who she said told her about the astral light where all things are stored. Theosophical doctrines define Akasha as a primordial substance through which all things arise. Although Blavatsky never mentioned the term "Akashic Records" directly, her writings influenced other Theosophical writers and followers to expand on her awareness in later years.

- *Henry Steele Olcott* (1832–1907): Along with Blavatsky, Olcott co-founded the Theosophical Society and mentioned the concept of the Akashic realm in his 1881 book, *Buddhist Catechism*.

- *Alfred Percy Sinnett* (1840–1921): The Theosophical follower became the first person to use the term "Akashic Records" in his book, *Esoteric Buddhism* (1883), citing that Buddhists described the records and believed people could read them if properly attuned to the spiritual path.

- *Annie Besant* (1847–1933): Former president of the original Theosophical Society in India, prolific Besant wrote of the Akashic Records.

- *Charles Webster Leadbeater* (1854–1934): Theosophist Leadbeater's 1899 book, *Clairvoyance,* discussed Akashic Records and claimed that anyone with clairvoyant talent could read them.

- *Rudolf Steiner* (1861–1925): Well-known Theosophist and philosopher Rudolf Steiner acknowledged an intricate connection between the physical and spiritual worlds in his many books. He believed physical matter left behind traces in the spiritual world. After a split with the Theosophical society, Steiner founded the Anthroposophy movement.

- *Alice A. Bailey* (1880–1949): Theosophy follower Alice Bailey spoke widely of the Akashic Records in her fascinating books and writings.

THE COLLECTIVE UNCONSCIOUS AND CARL GUSTAV JUNG (1875–1961)

What if all time is now and you and I are connected to the collective thought of all beings? That's what Swiss psychiatrist Carl Jung believed. Jung's Collective Unconscious theory suggests a giant thoughtform exists that all people tap into to share information through archetypes, shared memories, and experiences that are common to us all. Jung believed dream imagery and imagination made this information widely available to everyone and helped define how we collectively identify with universal concepts and ideas. He seemed to be describing that same Akashic realm touted by Blavatsky, Cayce, and others—that same space I call Mindstream. Did Jung tune into the wellspring of common data in the Akashic Records to find his ideas? I believe he did.

SLEEPING PROPHET EDGAR CAYCE
(1877–1945)

The father of holistic medicine and sleeping prophet Edgar Cayce is among the best-known people who masterfully accessed and named the Akashic Records during his lifetime. After a long illness, young Edgar Cayce went to a hypnotherapist for relief and went so deeply into a trance, he channeled an energy referred to as "Source." Strangely, Cayce could not recall a word he said during his sessions, so the information was preserved by observers. Cayce brought forth information on everything from health and wellness to past lives and future predictions. Considered the most documented psychic of the twentieth century, Cayce gave a staggering 14,000 individual life readings to clients all over the world.

Source revealed Cayce's prior incarnations in Egypt and Atlantis, and Cayce predicted three sets of Akashic Records would be discovered in Bimini, the Yucatán, and under the right paw of the Sphinx in Giza. Although no records have emerged from Egypt, x-ray technology suggests something is definitely under the Sphinx's right paw, yet the Egyptian government won't grant permission to access the area. Scientists uncovered what appeared to be a human-made road in Bimini, Bahamas, giving credence to Cayce's idea that at least part of the lost civilization of Atlantis remains buried under the sea in that area. If eventually proven, such discoveries would destroy our current understanding of perceived historical events and shatter our current understanding of humanity. Historically, Cayce made a major impact on our understanding of the Akashic Records by widely exposing the subject in popular culture.

BABA VANGA (1911–1996)

Considered the Nostradamus of the Balkans, the blind Bulgarian mystic Baba Vanga made startling predictions about events happening in modern times, including the 9/11 terrorist attacks on the World Trade Center.[4] With such precision and no logical means of where this information would have come from, we can only assume she accessed the Akashic Records.

ERVIN LASZLO (1932–)

Renowned Hungarian physicist Ervin Laszlo is author of numerous books on the concept of the Akashic Records and believes our current worldview is wrong. Thought and spirit create reality and give rise to our physical world, rather than the other way around. Everything we see and experience is a projection of the unseen reality. Experience and perception are secondary to the dynamic yet unseen spiritual field.

IMPORTANT BOOKS, DOCUMENTS, AND HISTORICAL RECORDS RELATING TO THE AKASHIC RECORDS

In addition to the historical figures who contributed to our modern collective understanding of the Akashic Records, the widespread belief in the concept of Akasha is evidenced in several ancient cultures and civilization, including the Mayans, Druids, and Meso-

4. Ritu Singh, "From 'Great Disasters & Cataclysms' to Cancer Cure: Here are Blind Mystic Baba Vanga's Predictions for 2021," India .com. Accessed January 1, 2021 https://www.india.com/viral/2021 -predictions-great-disasters-to-cancer-cure-here-are-blind-mystic-baba -vangas-predictions-for-2021-4289919/.

potamians, to name a few. Through the ages, cultures around the world shared a widespread belief in the idea of a record containing of all of humankind's deeds. This next section is a partial list of some of the more fascinating examples.

Egyptian Book of the Dead

The Egyptian Book of the Dead yields clues to the idea of a sacred collection of deeds that are recorded for all to witness. In order to enter into the afterlife, aspirants were required to greet forty-two gods and goddesses and offer forty-two negative confessions to Ma'at, the goddess of truth and wisdom. Unlike the typical Western concept of confessing to things you did, Egyptians had to declare what they did *not* do. After negatively confessing, the deceased would have their heart weighed on the scale of Ma'at, where any deception would be immediately revealed, as if recorded in some celestial place so that only the gods and the person themselves would know the real truth about their misdeeds. Interestingly, depictions of some of the Pharaohs in papyrus drawings show helpers tipping the scales in favor of their pharaoh, lest the weighing process didn't go their way.

Egyptian priests supposedly accessed otherworldly realms in order to advise the pharaohs. Priests in Memphis, for example, believed the god Ptah had a thoughtform in his heart that he expressed through his spoken word to create the world. This concept is akin to Laszlo's theories that the unseen world gives rise to waking reality.

Tibetan Book of the Dead

The Tibetan Book of the Dead describes interdimensional states of beings called *bardos* between life and death.[5] Tibetans believed that one should prepare for death during their lifetimes in order to achieve a more favorable afterlife and future reincarnation. Death is seen as transitional, not an end to being. It is instead an ascension into a higher state of consciousness that should be attained peacefully through meditative practice. Upon death, transitioning peacefully into the afterlife also helps yield a more favorable rebirth so the soul can avoid becoming trapped in undesirable and hellish bardo states. The acknowledgment of the continuation of consciousness through the Mindstream and the practice of projecting oneself into these intermediary states is a great example of accessing the Akashic realm. I've always viewed past-life regression as a great tool for experiencing death in past lives and feeling the spiritual freedom found in the space in between because this is as close to a real firsthand experience of the continuation of the soul after death that any of us can have. Such firsthand awareness brings greater peace to you while you're still alive, just as the Buddhists believe.

Biblical Revelation and Book of Life

Mentioned numerous times throughout the Bible, the book of life contains names of those fortunate souls who will enter the kingdom of heaven upon death. The Old Testament first describes this idea in Exodus 32:33: "Yet now, if thou wilt forgive their sin, and if not, blot me, I pray thee, out of thy book which thou hast written.

---

5. Matt Stefon, "Bardo Thödol," *Encyclopedia Britannica,* October 16, 2015: https://www.britannica.com/topic/Bardo-Thodol. Accessed February 2021.

And the Lord said unto Moses, Whoever hath sinned against me, him I will blot out of my book."

Old Testament writers mention this book of records several times, including Isaiah, Nehemiah, Job, Daniel, as well as:

- Jeremiah 17:1 calls the book a "tablet of their heart."
- Malachi 3:16 describes a "book of remembrance."
- Several times in Psalms, including when David explains, "… in thy book all my members were written …" (Psalm 139:16)

The New Testament also references the book of life several times:

- Apostle Paul described the "book of life" in Philippians 4:3.
- Luke 10:20 tells believers: "your names are written in heaven."

Perhaps the most notable discussion of this the book of life is found in Revelation 20:12.[6] John warns the book will open at judgment and those who find their names in the book will be admitted into the kingdom of heaven, while anyone missing from the book will not ascend in the afterlife:

"And I saw the dead, small and great, stand before God; and the books were opened: and another book was opened, which is the book of life: and the dead were judged out of those things which were written in the books, according to their works."

Thinking of predictive forecasts of future events, there is no better example than John's book of Revelation. Whether these

---

6 . Bible, King James Standard Version.

events ever happen or not, where might such predictions come from if not from the Akashic Records?

The Talmud

The Jewish Talmud mentions three books that would be opened in heaven. The first includes the wicked, the second the righteous, and the third lists everyone else. Yet another one of many examples of records kept of deeds great and small.

Hinduism and the Vedas

The Vedic concept of the *pancha mahabhutas* refers to the five elements: *akash* is considered the primary element of space, followed by *vayu* (air), *agni* (fire), *jala* (water), and *prithvi* (earth). The Theosophical Society acknowledged Indian mystics in their writings and discovered the akash through Hindu texts, expanding on the idea of an expansive void from which matter emerges. The Vedas and the holy Sanskrit language itself were believed to have been transcribed directly from the Akashic Records.

Plato's Timaeus and Aristotle

Greek philosopher Plato (ca. 427–ca. 347 BCE) is well known for first coining the term "element" and defining them in his *Timaeus* in geometrical patterns: fire as a tetrahedron, water as an icosahedron, air as an octahedron, and earth as a cube. These four sacred geometrical patterns came to be known as the Platonic solids. Philosophers argued and debated about the unseen force between the primary elements that remained unnamed. Eventually, Aristotle described what he called *aether*, the fifth element, that exists within the stars beyond earthly origins. Additionally, the Oracles at Delphi made predictions for luminaries that were widely regarded among the people. We can only speculate that these future events were foreseen within the Akashic Records.

SUMMING UP

Although there is no clinical scientific evidence or proof of the Akashic Records' existence, without a doubt the widespread belief in the etheric storehouse of information so prevalent across time and cultures around the world suggests such a place is very real indeed. Next, you will go through a series of steps and exercises to prepare you to access the Mindstream for yourself.

Chapter Two

BELIEF AND AREAS
OF EXPLORATION

Among my main goals for writing this book is to help you understand that the Akashic Records are much more than documents housed in some celestial library. These records contain every thought about every single thing in the entire universe: past, present, and future. There's no limit to the wisdom and information you can uncover by accessing the Akashic Records. To find the Akashic Records requires you to properly enter the inner-dimensional realm that we will call the Mindstream, which should be regarded as non-linear, formless, and limitless space. At the same time, we're going to need to create constructs that allow us mere mortals to work within this cosmic soup by likening parts of the Mindstream to things we know and understand in our earthly lives. One of the easiest ways to do that is to perceive the Akashic Records as books in a library, files in a storage cabinet, documents in your computer, and so forth.

Not only do we as individuals store our own records in this ethereal plane, so does everyone else. All things that have ever been thought, experienced, or created, now, in the past, future, or in any other dimension can be accessed through the Akashic Records. This book will help you understand what doors to open to receive various kinds of information. Each chapter introduces new areas you may want to explore. To start, let's take a look at some of the most common kinds of information you can access in the Mindstream.

SOUL'S PURPOSE

Our souls are like good books with overall arching themes that run like threads through all our lifetimes. In past-life regression work, I usually take my clients to (at minimum) two or three of their past lives. One of the big takeaways clients receive is the higher understanding of who they were in the past, and more importantly, how they can use the information to become happier in the now by identifying and following their soul's purpose or theme. By working within the relaxed space within the Mindstream and asking the right questions, clients uncover underlying themes or lessons that keep showing up for them lifetime after lifetime. Likewise, when you're accessing the records for yourself (which you will do a bit later in the book), one of the most beneficial pieces of information you'll find there that can help you enjoy greater peace and tranquility in your life is the deep recognition that your soul did show up in earthly form over many lifetimes and perhaps over hundreds—if not thousands—of years in order to fulfill a certain set of tasks and achieve a dominant purpose. There's no mistaking about it: you are here for a reason! You may not always understand why things happen as they do; believe me, nobody does. Yet through perseverance and a little self-analysis, you can emerge from the Mindstream with a greater understanding of who you truly are and know with great certainty that your life does indeed have a purpose.

We all want to find greater peace and meaning in our lives and the level of understanding you'll receive about yourself will give you a strong knowing that your life events are not as random as you might think. You're here for a definite reason; the people you've met, the circumstances you've encountered, the ups, the downs, all of it is crafted in a way that will help you achieve the goals your soul set out to experience during your lifetime.

We have so much stress and challenge in our lives—I know I have, and so have my clients. Every person alive has difficulties. What those hardships entail varies depending on the purpose. Everybody wants to feel like they're part of something bigger and as though the trials and tribulations they're going through will yield a positive outcome, even in the midst of adversity. Accessing my own records gave me peace about many things that have happened in my current life. By giving yourself permission to really experience yourself at the soul level without all the judgment and regret we often pile on ourselves, I hope you will emerge with a greater level of self-understanding, love, and acceptance.

PRESENT LIFE HEALING

There are many doorways in the Mindstream that you can go through to heal all kinds of situations that life throws at you. You can visit places of great peace; bathe in transformational healing light; and engage in meaningful conversations with ascended masters, angels, guides, your ancestors, or your own higher self. You can also connect with other people and their higher selves in your current lifetime so you can find resolution for deep issues that need to be healed and transformed.

If you're like so many people who are dealing with unresolved grief, that's among the most beneficial reasons to take a trip into the Mindstream. While there, you can have visionary experiences with those who you've loved and lost. You can forgive those who have wronged you, or apologize to people for things that happened in the past. There's simply no limit to what you can resolve within the Mindstream—and take it from me, you will reap great rewards by diving into these high-frequency places.

PAST LIVES

Accessing the Akashic Records helps you discover your past lives. The Mindstream contains so much incredibly useful information including a summary of many of your most meaningful and important past incarnations. Past-life regression is the main means I use to help my clients access their own soul records and discover their soul history, and later in the book, you'll have the chance to do go through several guided journeys designed to take you straight into your past-life memories.

I believe that we've lived so many lifetimes that the past lives that emerge will be those which are most beneficial for your highest good at any moment in time. One constant in our lives is the fact that with each nanosecond, the world is shifting, rotating, and evolving. You, too, are in constant flux in the universal flow of time. For that reason, each instance of inquiry will likely bring up the themes you're going through at the moment you make that observation. The information always comes so you can receive what will most benefit you at any given moment, and it's all perfect and in divine timing. For that reason, you may want to do journeys more than once, whenever you're guided.

GLOBAL TRENDS

In chapter one, we explored some of the many famous historical figures who were able to successfully access the areas within the Akashic Records that contain prophetic information and then provide those predictions to the general public. I'm not personally drawn to do this myself, but like them, it's theoretically possible that you too can go into the records to access details on overarching global patterns and future events. I believe that with knowledge comes great responsibility. Future predictions seem a bit daunting to me so I avoid it, but you may be different. Will it work for you? That remains to be seen.

Whenever dipping into the Mindstream, I've found that each soul brings forth certain kinds of information that's meant for them to discover. There's no forcing or coercing the information from the field. Some seers are meant to predict the future, while others are not. I don't believe it's my purpose, for example, to make predictions. The book has several kinds of exercises so that, after going through them, you can at some point learn not only what areas of these vast storehouses you want to explore but also which ones seem to come to you most naturally. We will be practicing how to open to the highest levels of light-filled information and to stay aligned with your own soul's purpose for what you're meant to do or not do during your time in the Akashic Records and within the Mindstream. The Akashic Records will always reveal what you're meant to know and what you're vibrationally aligned with at any given moment. Thanks to the constant flux and movement of the universe, that information is subject to change. We will discuss all of that as we move forward.

FUTURE MEMORIES

Speaking of global trends and the future, much of my work involves helping people access memories of their current life futures. Because the Mindstream is a multidimensional construct, there are unlimited possible outcomes for our future. In regression hypnosis, it's incredibly important to be neutral and help clients discover their own information without the therapist trying to lead them with questions or tone.

Current life future memories are different. Because all possible realities are coexisting in time and space, I listen to my clients and we do our past explorations by tuning into the details regarding whatever issue they came to me to address. For example, if they wanted to heal a relationship, which is an incredibly common challenge for so many, then we would travel into the past so they could receive wisdom from their own higher self, guides, or past-life recollection. Once we do that, I ask them to go out into the future to a happy place where everything regarding the current challenge has been successfully resolved and they're feeling peaceful, healthy, and vibrant. It's interesting to note that I've never, ever had a person who couldn't go to their happy place. Why? Because that place in time exists as a possible reality as sure as any other. Why not choose the best possible outcome for ourselves?

The other interesting aspect of these future memories is that clients can come to an understanding of the exact step-by-step details of how they came to create this wonderful life for themselves because in the space they're at in that future place, *the events have already happened.* Clients experience a kind of reverse engineering of the soul to see and experience the steps they need to follow—the recipe for success, if you will. The real challenge then becomes what they choose to do after our session has ended. Will they listen to themselves and pursue their dreams? Will they follow the roadmap their soul put before them? That's all up to them, of course, but in many cases they do, and they reap the benefits of positive living as a result.

Later in the book, you will have a chance to go to a bright future event and learn how to co-create your reality by accessing your brightest possible future in the Mindstream.

PARALLEL UNIVERSES AND
THE MULTIVERSE

Almost twenty years ago, I began asking questions and created processes to help clients grappling with some of the weirder aspects of life that defy logical explanation by guiding them into a space where they could find out if they existed in parallel realities; many reported simultaneous lives.

Back then, I firmly believed (and still do) that you and I can create the life we want by changing our thinking and shifting awareness. My research suggests that we can spontaneously recall our past lives without even going into a trance or hypnosis. I developed a term, Supretrovie, after discovering that everyone has these flashes of insight into their former selves and can receive this information through very little effort.

Daily life can also be influenced by experiences of past, present or future. We time travel constantly through these unconscious shifts in awareness. The best way I can demonstrate this is to ask you think about what you're going to be having for lunch today. Take a moment now and go to the future. Think for just a second about your midday meal. Notice the first thought that pops into your mind. Make a mental note of that and see what happens.

Now, take a moment to think back to a toy you loved as a child. Notice what thought pops into your mind. Do you see it? Can you feel it? Great! You just time traveled into the future and into the past! We can easily shift our inner focus and go into past and future events with or without going into a meditative state. Of course guided imagery helps, but it's not always necessary. We receive intuitive flashes and insights every moment of every single day, and those impulses are influencing us in untold ways. What if these insights are flowing in from the Mindstream, from the Akashic realm? I believe they are.

By shifting your awareness into the Akashic realm, you will be able to develop the ability to easily access the information you need from the Mindstream and greatly enhance your innate intuitive ability along the way. It's all there existing simultaneously and only requires a slight shift in awareness to access. Through guided imagery, you will be able to consciously decide which aspects of this multiverse you want to tune into to bring you information for your highest good. You'll be introduced to some interesting exercises to help you tune into these multidimensional aspects of yourself.

BENEFITS OF ACCESSING
THE AKASHIC RECORDS

Aside from the numerous places we can visit via the Mindstream, accessing the Akashic Records can be hugely beneficial and life-changing for several reasons, including the following:

Smoother Flow of Life: A long time ago, I discovered that by following the loving inner guidance that is coming to you at all times, you can find happiness. Likewise, by listening to your inner guidance, your life becomes infinitely easier.

Receive Actionable Communication from Your Higher Self: All people have the answers within them about how to best proceed and what to do to create greater happiness and harmony in their lives. Learning to tune in to the Mindstream will help you move forward with greater certainty, knowing your actions are those that will be in the best interests of all concerned and will contribute to your overall soul growth and happiness. This book will take you into spaces where you will find clear answers that are tailormade for you and you alone.

Create Greater Peace: When you open to your own inner wisdom, you become one with the flow of the divine; in that, your life begins to work better.

Eliminate Confusion: With all the choices we have in modern times, you'd think people would be happier, but they're not. Why? Having everything at your fingertips one hundred percent of the time brings up a new dilemma for the modern seeker—what should I be doing/watching/reading at any given moment? Learning to tune in to your higher wisdom and spirit guide helps you make decisions throughout the day about what activities you should focus on that would bring greater peace to your life.

I've really struggled with listening to this wisdom myself; I have tons of ideas floating in and know my time is limited. I used to spend a lot of energy being overwhelmed by what to do or which order to do things in. That's when I turned to different tools discussed in the exercises section to help you get hold of the things that will help you avoid confusion and move forward with clarity.

Discernment: With all those choices, another benefit of tuning in to the Mindstream is to choose the best path for yourself that will be for your highest good. All the answers you need are within you. Developing intuition and accessing the

Akashic Records helps you understand how you best receive that guidance.

SUMMING UP

The Akashic Records and Mindstream yield unlimited potential for you to expand your awareness of your purpose. There's no telling how you'll be able to enhance your life by following the wisdom found in the Akashic Records.

Chapter Three

CREATING SACRED SPACE AND PREPARING FOR THE MINDSTREAM

Before you can begin accessing the Akashic Records, you will want to prepare yourself by creating a sacred space where you can do your work and become clear on your intentions. This kind of preparation applies to guided journeys, energy healing, or any other type of spiritual work you're planning to do. The effort you make here can yield amazing results down the road.

Setting up a space where you sit every time you do your work creates a mini-vortex of positive, high vibrations. The more you sit in meditation or prayer and work in the energy, the easier it will be to go there. In general, your surroundings can cue your subconscious mind on the spiritual significance of what you're about to go through, just based on where you choose to set up.

As for how to decorate your space, the sky's the limit. You may like pleasant music or tonal sounds, you may enjoy lighting candles or incense before you begin. Choose any personal touches you enjoy that make you feel connected to the divine. Again, over time, even the smell of a certain essential oil, candle, or incense can trigger your subconscious mind to access these other realms. As always, these are personal choices, so there's no right or wrong.

The idea is to create the space to get the energy flowing. Through practice and repetition, those energies increase over time. We will dig deeper into some ideas in this chapter to give you inspiration as you go along.

SEATING AND SHAKTI

Whenever you're doing guided journeys, you will obviously need to sit or recline in a comfortable place. I recommend using the same chair every time because that will help your subconscious mind attune to your spiritual work. You will be able to move deeper within the Mindstream when you're comfortable. Any space used repeatedly for meditation or journeys builds up *shakti*, a Hindu term referring to primordial spiritual vibrations. I use a chair that I've come to refer to as the *chair of trance* because it's the same place I've been sitting for twenty years during my meditations and while working with my clients. The moment I sit there, I can go immediately into a meditative state and feel lovely tingling energy all around me.

Ideally, you'll want to pick a place where you won't be disturbed that's quiet and private, a place you enjoy where you can let your guard down and feel safe. Once you pick your special spot, fill the area with items that make you feel supported. You may also want to keep blankets or pillows around because your body temperature can often fluctuate when you sit in trance.

MUSIC, CANDLES, GEMSTONES, INCENSE, AND OILS

Vibrational remedies create actual changes in the energy fields within and around the body, as well as within a sacred space. These tools provide an easy way to help you shift energy in your space to prepare for spiritual work. A few of my favorites are included here.

Music

Music is incredibly healing to the soul. Pick calming music you enjoy and either play it before you sit down to shift the vibrations in your space, or use the music along with your guided journeys. Artists such as Jonathan Goldman and Steven Halpern create alpha wave music that automatically puts your brainwaves into the trance state. If you venture to YouTube, you can find tons of pioneers experimenting with music that may support physical wellbeing simply through listening. Check the resources section for more details.

Candles

Calling upon the transformative fire element with candles can set the space for working within the Akashic Records. Scents such as cinnamon or lavender can be supportive too, but if you're sensitive to smells, unscented may be the best option. You can also evoke the fire element with battery-operated candles. Even if the flame is artificial, the intent is still there.

Gemstones and Crystals

Do you have favorite stones or crystals? You may want to keep them close and hold them during your journeys. Crystals can help to amplify frequencies and create the energy to allow you to move deeper into your work. Above all, remember to select whatever stone feels good to you in the moment, and always defer to your own intuition. Pick favorites to support you energetically on your path. A few popular choices include:

- Amethyst—vibrates at the same frequency as the violet ray and helps open up the third eye to enhance psychic journeys and mystical experiences
- Clear quartz—works as an amplifier and will help you run energy through the body as you prepare to enter the Mindstream
- Tourmaline—a grounding stone that protects your field from unwanted influences

Sage

Burning bundled sage is one of my favorite ways to shift frequencies in a space. You can walk room to room to clear unwanted energies and run the smoke over your body to ritualistically clear yourself before you begin.

Incense

Incense also shifts your vibrations and can trigger your subconscious mind to expand into the spiritual realm. A personal favorite is nag champa, a sandalwood-based incense that instantly lifts the vibrations in your space and sets the tone for trance states. Experiment and use what you enjoy best!

Essential Oils

Small drops of essential oils are incredible for instantly changing your state from stress to relaxation and wellness. Lavender vibrates at a high frequency aligned with the violet ray and helps the third eye open so you can receive divine wisdom. Diffusers will allow you to use the oil frequencies in your space to immediately shift your energy.

Flower Essences

The best are Bach Flower Remedies, which bottle up the holographic imprints of flowers to allow you to benefit from their high frequency, loving vibrations. A couple of drops can shift your field in an instant! Rescue Remedy is a favorite for healers.

Symbol Based Energy Healing

Another interesting way to clear the entire room you're in before settling down for your journey work is by sending positive energy directly into your space. To do this, follow these steps:

1. Imagine feeling a sensation of energy moving through the top of your head, through your arms, and out the palms of your hands. You may feel this sensation or you could use your inner vision to know the energy is moving from head to hands. As you notice this flow, send the energy into the room. You may feel tingling sensations in the hands, or you may simply intend this is happening and know the energy is moving into your space and clearing any unwanted influences. Feel your room filling up with pure love and light.

2. Next, consider the corners. Turn and face each of the four corners while sending energy from your hands. Imagine through your inner vision that positive flow is enlivening your room.

3. Spin slowly in a circle with your arms fully stretched out and your palms facing the walls. Circle around a few times, imagining a strong flow of positivity emerging into your room.

4. As the light moves from your hands, continue sending this energetic flow until you sense your whole room is filled with positive love and light. Sense that a protective layer of light is surrounding you and your proceedings.

***

Intention is key. Set the intention that you are creating a harmonious space for yourself and allow yourself to bask in the loving and supportive energy. Trust that you successfully created the proper energy for your space.

CREATING YOUR ALTAR

Once you've selected and cleared your space, you may want to create an altar where you can work. Altars are nothing more than places where you can focus your intention on your spiritual nature. Your altar doesn't have to be complicated; I have a couple of altars on bookshelves in my home where I placed candles and statues I enjoy such as my many Buddhas and other deities I've collected through my travels over the years. I don't think it's necessary to do anything overly formal just so long as you enjoy the things you place there and they hold spiritual significance for you. My altar is not right next to my sitting space but is in the same room. Assuming you've picked your special sacred place where you'll be meditating and working and you've cleared the air with whatever tools you've chosen, you will want to take the following steps before you sit down to begin any journey work:

Exercise

1. Stand in quiet contemplation before your altar.

2. Quiet your mind.

3. Breathe. Breathing in through the nose will relax the nervous system and open you to receive.

4. Tune in to your body and ask yourself a couple of questions: How do I feel? What places are tense within my body? What unwanted emotions come to mind that I can clear before I begin?

5. If you feel tension, breathe into those areas, and if needed, use the vibrational remedy of your choice to shift your energy and then return to your altar and follow the steps again of quieting the mind and tuning in until you feel clear and ready to begin.

6. Take a moment to express gratitude. Life is challenging, but at any given time, there's always something you can feel grateful about.

7. Concentrate on what you have to be thankful for and allow that feeling to expand into your body. Take your time until you can physically feel greater peace in every single area of your body before you continue with your spiritual work.

***

One of the big challenges with these exercises is remembering to do them in the first place. If you miss a day, don't worry. If you have trouble finding something inspiring to be grateful for, don't beat yourself up. Be where you are at any given moment and have compassion for yourself and your journey.

CLEARING YOURSELF OF UNWANTED INFLUENCES

Once you're done clearing the room and preparing using your favorite tools, another way you can ensure that you are clear and ready for connecting with the Mindstream is by clearing unwanted influences from your field. Whether you consider yourself highly sensitive or not, there's no doubt that you're picking up the vibes from people around you. I've found it's imperative to make sure you're not being unduly influenced by the outer world before ever attempting to tap into your own inner council. Every single person alive has the ability to tune in to what's best for them, but it can be super challenging when we're not even aware of how much other people are influencing us. I don't mean that people are doing so in any malicious way; we simply sense other people by being around each other. Ultimately, you want what's best for you, so clearing yourself in this way before sitting down to consider important matters is vital. What follows is a brief exercise I use daily that will help you tremendously.

Exercise

Stand near your altar. Acknowledge that there is an invisible energy or cord that connects you with all things and people in the universe. Imagine an invisible pair of scissors or a golden sword that sweeps down the front of your body, down your back, both sides, as well as the soles of your feet and the top of your head. Imagine the scissors or sword cutting the cords between you and all other influences so you are not energetically affected by the outer world or other people any longer. Once the cords are cut, you are fully yourself, free and clear and ready to open to your own higher wisdom. Once you've done this process, feel yourself standing there and imagine you can notice a significant shift in your energy which should feel like a slight increase in your own personal field after the cords are cut. See or imagine yourself clear of any unwanted psychic or mental energy of others. Imagine you are free to be exactly who you are in this moment, and accept this moment.

During this procedure, you may see people, places, or things that emerge in your mind's eye as you cut the cords. Allow those thoughts, feelings, and images to be what they are without judgment. Then again, you may not see anything when these cords are cut. In fact, you don't need to know exactly what you're cutting cords with at all. Just accept that it's happening in accordance with your highest good and acknowledge that you feel better as a result. The things you're cutting cords with could be positive or negative. The point is to be free of outside influences so you can bask in your true self and become better prepared to receive guidance that is for your highest good. Take as long as you need to do this process; when you feel complete, continue about your day.

***

How did you do? This process does not have to take more than a minute or two. Remember also that it's not important to always know exactly what you're freeing yourself from, but rather the intention is to get back to the essence of who you are, to align with your own higher self so you will be ready to receive information that is truly in your best interest without the influences of others. Another variant on this process is to enlist a special guide to assist you with this cord cutting. Later in chapter 5, you will meet with your guides so, once you do that, you could always ask them to assist you if you're guided to do so. Either way, the process is meant to empower you to fully embrace your own inner wisdom.

CRAFTING AREAS OF INQUIRY

The other big piece of advice I must share with you involves discernment, one of the most important skills you can develop in your lifetime. Discernment refers to how to pick and choose one thing over another, and sadly, in this modern instant gratification society we live in, I think this skill is needed now more than ever before. How will you learn to discern what's best for you so you will enquire only about those items that will make the biggest positive impact on your life? Simple!

Exercise

Once you've set the room and cut the cords with the outer world, you're now ready to begin considering what you want to work on.

Exercise

Pull out a piece of old-fashioned paper and make a list of issues or items you would like to gain clarity on within the Mindstream. If you're not one who uses physical paper, that's fine too. Just type a short list in your phone or on your device that you can read and refer to during this exercise. There's no need to overthink or edit your list at all, because we're going to weed out the unimportant items with the next step. Just allow yourself to free flow with ideas that occur to you in the moment. Pay attention to the first thoughts that pop into your mind and write it all down. Take your time.

***

When I do this, invariably, some of these thoughts are random ideas I won't be pursuing at all, but it's so helpful to at least take note of these thoughts because too many can become quite confusing. You will want to achieve great clarity of intention before ever stepping into the Mindstream.

MUSCLE TESTING FOR CLARITY

Once your list of seemingly random thoughts is complete, it's time to test to see what is actually for your highest good.

Exercise

Take the list you wrote down and place that list in front of you. Find a heavy object to use as a tool. I use a metal trivet (used for placing a hot pan on a table) that I bought years ago. It's heavy enough for me to know it's working but not so heavy that it's difficult to use.

Hold your arm out straight while holding your item and prepare to ask questions. Know that if the answer to your question is an affirmative yes, you will be able to easily lift your arm, regardless of how heavy your item seems. If the answer is a negative no or something you should not pursue, you will be physically unable to lift the object from the table or space where it's sitting, even if it's light as a feather.

First, you must ask permission to make this inquiry. I like to say: "It's okay to ask these questions." If my arm lifts, then I assume that answer is yes and proceed. If my arm does not lift, it's a no. If for some reason you do receive a no, it's not okay to ask questions, then stop and come back later and try again. Usually, it's okay to ask questions though, so I think you should get a yes answer on that most of the time, if not always.

Next, create a practice question to further test the strength of your connection with your higher self. I always use "Is my name Shelley?" Obviously that's a question I can easily get an affirmative read on. Once I establish the feeling of receiving a positive answer, I ask another question: "Is my name is George?" Of course I will receive a negative answer on that, so if the muscle testing is working correctly, this should cause me to be completely unable to lift my trivet. In reality, I wouldn't be able to lift a feather either because when I say things that are untrue, my muscles weaken. Yours will be the same, and you can use any questions you'd like to test, but the name questions work particularly well for this intention.

Now that you've established your baseline for a positive or negative answer, go through the list you made earlier. Point to one item at a time, and state the following: "It is in my best interest to look into this item." If it's a yes, your hand will lift, and if it's a no, you won't be able to move your arm. I like using positive language here by asking about my highest good. We always want our highest good when doing anything. As you go through the items, you can either cross items off the list entirely or circle the ones that you want to pursue.

At times, you may have something on your list that on a conscious level, you really wanted to pursue. You may be shocked or surprised by the lack of muscle strength when inquiring about something you felt strongly about and you may have a hard time accepting the answers you receive. I say this because it's happened to me! It's quite difficult at times to let go of intentions that our higher self does not feel is for our highest good. I've had certain inquiries I've made over the years that did not give me the answer I wanted to hear. If that happens to you, feel free to do what I've done in the past—ask again. You could ask again and again if you're so inclined and can see if the answer ever changes to a positive. When that happened to me, I must have requestioned myself a hundred times or more. At some point, like me, you'll have to come to terms with the truth, even though you may not understand or like the answer.

I've had to learn over the years that when I do not follow my inner guidance, things can go spectacularly wrong! I don't want that to happen to you. I've come to truly trust and believe in my inner guidance and place more value in this kind of inquiry than any reading I could ever receive from a talented psychic or astrologer. Why? Because this is my own wisdom guiding me. Once I finally became tired of having things go awry, I honored this guidance and followed it, even when it wasn't what I consciously thought I wanted to do. I avoided what I shouldn't do, and I pursued the things that had a positive muscle test. I assure you, my life is running smoother than ever thanks to my new way of being. Do what you will, but at the end of the day, like me, you'll have the choice put before you quite clearly. Do you trust yourself or not? It's all up to you! The wisdom that comes from within is the best advice you can ever receive.

Once you've narrowed down what you will do and what you will put aside, you can also use this process to establish an order. "It's in my best interest to do this first," and so on, until you receive clarity about your priorities. If one of the list items received a no right now, another point is that you could put it aside and ask again down the road a bit. It's possible that at a later time, some of those activities may be valid and worth pursuing. Timing is everything though, as they say, so ensure your actions are happening when they're for your highest and best.

***

Practice this and see what emerges for you. Over time, you may find that like me, your life runs smoother than before.

PRAYERS AND AFFIRMATIONS

Some practitioners may enjoy saying a prayer, reciting a sacred text, or declaring a positive affirmation before beginning their personal journey work. I do not always say my prayers aloud; often I simply think of them and set the intentions that way. The prayer I always use is:

"I'm calling in my guides, ascended masters, and any beings of love and light who wish to join me today for this healing journey. May Higher Will be done!"

At the end of my sessions, I say the following:

"Please allow this healing to continue. May Higher Will be done!"

***

Because of the etheric nature of energy, healing can continue to extend light and benefits long after a session has ended. Setting your intention that healing will continue when closing your sessions lets the universal manager know that you aim to receive residual benefits for hours, days, weeks, or even years afterward while allowing greater light, peace, and joy to move into every area of your life.

PSYCHIC PROTECTION

The guided imagery exercises you'll find throughout this book are purposefully designed to put you inside a protective shield, which I recommend for any kind of healing work. If you would like to state such an intention aloud, you could say something like: "I ask that only that which is of love and light come through." We kind of already intended that in the last section on prayer by asking for our highest good, but again whatever wording or ritual you believe will assist you is fine. Once you set the firm intention that only that which is of love and light can come through, you will always attract positive outcomes. Always remember that your intention is the most important aspect of any spiritual work.

Along with the protective and loving presence of your personal spirit guide, the journeys themselves will also be a comfort and provide psychic protection. Each exercise will ask you to draw upon a healing white universal light and place yourself inside a golden protective ball. I find the golden light is incredibly protective and comforting, both for myself and my clients. This kind of relaxation not only serves to open up your energy to the divine but also ensures you are met by the highest frequency beings and realms possible.

RECORDING JOURNEYS

I always recommend students and readers record their journeys, which is easy to do these days because there are so many recording apps you can download on your phone. If you invest a little bit of extra time to actually read these journeys aloud and record them, you can use them any time you'd like to receive optimal results. And although many of us detest listening to ourselves, believe it or not, your subconscious mind loves listening to your voice. The effort will be well worth it!

DOCUMENT YOUR PROGRESS IN A JOURNAL

Another constant recommendation I must make is to suggest you get a journal to document the progress you're making with the exercises in this book. Any kind of journal is fine. You can either use a paper journal or some kind of word document or app where you can create a file or section specifically for this book. The real goal is to jot down all the epiphanies you will hopefully receive from going into these multiple dimensions within the Mindstream. I've been keeping journals for years now, and I never know when something I wrote down ten or more years ago will come in handy. Again, it takes only a couple of extra minutes to do so, but the rewards can be staggering and imperative to your life journey to help you navigate through the various twists and turns to achieve your highest degree of happiness, peace and harmony. At the end of the day, the only reason to do any of this work in the first place is to create deeper levels of contentment for your life. I pray this material will help you achieve those ends!

SUMMING UP

Creating sacred space where you feel comfortable and supported is highly recommended when working within the Akashic Records. Once you get ready to go on any journey, above all else, your *intention* is what matters. We'll be moving into the guided journeys soon, and each one will have a place built in for you to state the intentions of what you're looking for so you will emerge with whatever is best for your highest good.

Next, we will expand our discussion by looking at how to create protective shields of light around you while working and how to make the divine connection that will allow you to access the Akashic Records within the Mindstream.

Chapter Four

OPENING THE DOOR
TO THE MINDSTREAM

My ideas of what the Akashic Records are and how you're going to navigate them did not come from reading books but rather through my own individual experiences and after working with clients over many years of private practice. The Mindstream is comprised of a series of doorways in other dimensions you can walk through to access transformational information. In this chapter, you'll go through an expansive relaxation process and locate and walk through your very first door within the Mindstream. Before we begin to explore, there are a couple of key areas that will greatly enhance your ability to achieve your desired outcome from the Akashic Records.

SETTING YOUR INTENTION

In the last chapter, you did a series of exercises to help you become clear within yourself. Additionally, before venturing into the Mindstream it's incredibly important for you to set specific intentions each time you access that space for what you would like to receive there. I've built in places within the guided meditations where you will need to state your intentions; while you may recall them without much effort, you may also want to spend a little time thinking about what you intend to get from each journey. Stating your true intentions clearly is the best way to ensure positive results from any kind of spiritual work.

Think of it this way: if you go to the store without a list but only the intention to buy some vegetables, it's easy to suddenly find yourself exploring the bakery, buying things you don't need, and possibly forgetting why you went there in the first place. Life is the same way. A bit of conscious preparation goes a long way.

While intent is paramount to your success, there's another fine line we must discuss—avoid becoming too attached to how things show up. You want what you want, and yet things arrive in unexpected forms at times. A good example is that same trip to the store. Let's say you set your intention to buy vegetables. You had specifics in mind, but as you look around the produce section, you may be disappointed by things you couldn't find or may discover new items that you hadn't planned on. Journey work is the same. Our interior vision of what we can have and be in life is often influenced by our past experiences. What if there's something even more amazing awaiting you that you've never heard of before? Intent says that we don't want unexpected or unpleasant surprises, yet you want to be open to miracles and gifts of the spirit that far exceed your current expectations.

IMAGINATION

The importance of imagination to creating a meaningful life cannot be understated. The major key to accessing past lives and connecting with other dimensions is the ability to suspend criticism of the intuitive and often strange flashes of insight that pop into your mind when you receive higher wisdom and guidance.

The questions you will face in the Mindstream are often things you've never been asked before. Back in the early part of my career, I took classes for Practitioner and Master Practitioner of Neuro-Linguistic Programming (NLP), a modality invented in the 1970s by John Grinder and Richard Bandler that says your brain is like a computer. Need better results? Go in and reprogram the input to receive a better output. These training classes were a solid month each of intense work that proved to be some of the most valuable classes I've ever taken for helping me understand how people think and work as well as how to achieve optimal results in life.

In NLP, you learn to identify whether people are more visual, auditory/hearing, or kinesthetic/feeling. Identification helps you get along better with others and build friendship and rapport. I spent two solid months of my life very early in my career studying NLP, so I use some of its theories as the basis for my understanding of how people communicate, learn, and work together.

Following the idea that the brain is like a computer, an answer to any posed question will appear in the mind as a picture, thought, or feeling. Many times these images or thoughts seem absolutely nuts and are easy to dismiss. Allowing the imaginative part of yourself to emerge and going with the insights you receive without dismissal or judgment can lead to transformational insights. Believing in the miraculous wonders of the Divine and becoming comfortable enough to express new and unusual thoughts when they emerge while taking note of important insights after sessions can lead to real breakthroughs and healing. Because the Akashic Records are nonlinear, we must go there via guided imagery; many of those images may seem a little weird or may not make sense. By opening up to the imaginative part of your mind and your childlike curiosity and openness, you will succeed in accessing the dreamlike imagery of the Akashic realm.

HONOR YOUR INTUITIVE GIFTS

Speaking of pictures, thoughts, and feelings, those same categories apply to intuition. One of the best gifts you can give yourself by exploring the Mindstream is self-love and acceptance regarding your own unique brand of intuition by developing what comes naturally to you, while working to expand other areas where you'd like to become more proficient. For example, whenever people attend psychic development workshops, it always seems that there's at least one person in class who describes vivid visual details about all the amazing paranormal things they saw and encountered. This tends to leave other people who are less visual feeling like complete failures because they can't understand why information doesn't flow like that for them. I know this because that's how I used to feel when I attended these kinds of programs. Some people are super visual, and that's wonderful. Others are more auditory or able to hear an inner voice, while others, like me, tended to be more touchy feely. Believe it or not, when I first started doing guided journeys myself years ago, I didn't see a thing. I had to learn how to tap into feelings to get information; over time and through practice and repetition, I began developing my ability to hear information and eventually see things in my mind. So, just know that however it is that you bring in intuitive insights, you're perfect the way you are and it's all good! Accept yourself and from there, you can always do what I did and practice other means of receiving.

LISTENING TO YOUR OWN ADVICE

In the next chapter, we're going to go meet with your spirit guides and you will be moving into spaces where your guides and your own inner wisdom and higher self will give you advice. Asking our guides to help us or to give us information we need is common. But do we listen when we receive these priceless bits of wisdom? Maybe, maybe not. I always think of the cartoon about the man stranded in the water who asks God to rescue him from drowning. While he's busy focusing on the clouds, expecting a lightning bolt to zap him out of his predicament, several people appear. One brings a boat, and another shows up flying a helicopter over his head, yet he's ignoring them all, hanging on to the vision in his mind of some supernatural being coming to his rescue.

Believe it or not, your guides are the same: they're trying to communicate with you all the time. One goal for anyone wanting to open themselves up psychically would be to develop the means to receive the information relayed to us from our guides and helpers, something we will work on as we progress through these pages. For now, consider how you best receive intuitive information, and be honest about how well you've followed your own advice. I've spent quite a bit of my life not following these priceless bits of wisdom, I assure you, but I changed my ways once I realized how much better my life could become when I do. You can too—it just takes intention and practice.

RAISING VIBRATIONS AND INCREASING ENERGY FLOW

Consciously raising your vibrations and separating yourself from what I call unwanted influences is an important spiritual practice.

One of the best ways to do this is through a simple meditation to increase the flow of energy from your crown center located at the top of your head, through your body and feet. Once you make that connection and allow that high frequency light to move through your entire body, you will feel lighter and better than ever and more prepared to enter the Mindstream. It only takes a couple minutes, but it's incredibly helpful and a great place to start.

Exercise

Sit in a comfortable space with your feet flat on the floor. Close your eyes. Breathe and relax. Sense the soles of your feet, and feel them touching the floor. Imagine an energizing sensation can begin to move up from the earth through your feet and legs, into your torso, into your arms, hands and into your neck and head. Imagine that flow begins moving from head to feet, and feet to head. Imagine you can enliven your own flow of energy through your body and consciously will that energy to become stronger and stronger. Imagine every single cell in your body becomes lighter and lighter and lighter. Imagine noticing how your actual frequency can increase when you put your conscious intention on that outcome. Raise your frequency so high, higher and higher and higher, that any unwanted influences of a lower vibration will no longer affect you. Tune into the feeling of rising above limitations and existing in a space of total peace and oneness. Feel the incredibly high vibrations and align with those now. Very good! Continue for as long as you're guided. When you're ready, open your eyes and feel better than you did before.

***

How did that go? Awesome! Once you've increased the flow of energy running through your body, you can move to the next step.

CONNECTING TO ASTRAL LIGHT

In the spirit of Madame Blavatsky, we're going to call upon something we will refer to as the Astral Light. This exercise will serve to establish your starting point; from here, each progressive experience will build upon the other. In essence, I always guide clients and readers through relaxation before transitioning to a past-life regression or any other kind of healing. This Astral Light will be a bit different, though, because you're going to more consciously establish yourself and your energy field between heaven and earth to better facilitate your ability to access the Mindstream. Ready? Let's begin.

Exercise

Close your eyes and breathe. Find yourself now breathing in peace, healing, and relaxation. Feel the center of your head, and imagine that you notice a beam of pure white light moving down through the top of your head. Allow the light to move through your body toward your feet. As the light moves through you, notice if there is any tension in the body or anything troubling you now, and imagine the light can go into those places and wash away any challenges or darker areas. Imagine you can notice that as the light moves through your body toward your feet that your tension begins to fade and any dark or heavy spots are replaced by a peaceful, healing white light. Take your time as you totally agree to release all stress and tension now. Very good.

Now imagine you can feel the warmth of this light and imagine it has a loving, peaceful energy. Know that within this loving light you are always safe, secure, and totally at peace. Within this light, only the highest frequencies of love can come through. You are loved and you notice now that any pain, suffering, or discomfort disappears. Only peace and love remain. Go ahead and take your time as you allow this peaceful feeling to settle in over you. Feel the light moving into every single cell in your body, starting from the top of your head, to your arms and hands, your torso and legs, to your ankles, and all the way down to the soles of your feet and tips of your toes. Feel the loving light moving into every single cell in your body. Cells are opening, expanding and relaxing as you invite this pure white light to expand the light within you. Now that white light is moving back up from your feet, all the way up to the top of your head. Feel the light opening all the cells in the soles of your feet, your toes, your heels, and ankles. Feel this loving light moving up, up, up, and into your legs, through your calves, your knees and thighs. The light is expanding every single cell in the body. All cells are filling with this loving light now. That light is moving up, up, up, into your lungs. Breathe this peaceful light into your lungs. Now imagine the light moving through your stomach and up into your heart center. Allow that light to move into every cell of your heart, healing any pain, emotional or otherwise. Feel your heart light expand as you beam loving vibrations into the world. This light continues moving now, up, up, up, through your shoulder blades and into your neck and shoulders. The light moves into your arms and hands and fingers. The light continues opening all cells, filling your entire being with love and light as this light continues to travel all the way up through your neck, into your mouth and jaw, your nose, ears, forehead, and into your eyes. The light is getting stronger and stronger as it moves into the top of your head and pours out the crown of your head. Allow that pure white light to connect you with Source energy, the Universe, and the All That Is. Notice now that you're totally connected with Spirit or Source energy. Allow the unconditional love and peace of Spirit to emanate throughout your body.

Imagine you are standing in the exact center of heaven and earth. The white light pours down from Source, moves through the body, and bursts once again out the soles of your feet. That white light is moving down, down, down, to the very core of the earth, connecting you with Mother Earth and Father Sky. You are at the perfect center of All That Is. Feel connected to everything in the known universe in this sacred space and Astral Light.

Allow the Astral Light to pour forth from your heart center. As the light rushes out of your heart, the light begins to form a ball of golden healing light around you. Feel the loving vibrations of the golden light surrounding you by about three feet in all directions and know that within this golden light and with this pure white beam of Astral Light connecting you with heaven and earth, you are now totally safe, secure, and carefree. You know only that which is of your highest good can come through. Know that you can carry this Astral Light with you now and always. When you're ready, and when I count from three, you'll be back, feeling wide awake, refreshed, and better than ever before. Three, grounded, centered and balanced; two, keeping this peaceful feeling with you now and always; and one, you're back!

***

There are no words to emphasize the importance of knowing how to draw down Astral Light from above and shield yourself in the loving embrace of the universe. This process is something

I do for myself daily, and it doesn't even need to take as long as it does in the exercise you just did. All you need to do is close your eyes and instantaneously call in Astral Light to come through your head, quickly send it through the entire body and out your feet, and then imagine you can feel that light moving down into the core of the earth. Once you connect with the earth's core, imagine feeling the light moving back up through the body and sense your connection. You can do this in as little as thirty seconds. Once you get into the habit of connecting with Father Sky and Mother Earth and practice bringing Astral Light into your physical body, you will begin to feel greater levels of peace and calm, no matter what's happening in your outer world. The Astral Light intends a connection with only the highest beings of love and light available; it serves as a protective psychic shield by its very nature. I hope you will continue to do this process until it becomes a habit. This exercise is the foundation for everything else we're going to do together here, so I know you will find it gets easier and easier as you go along.

DOORWAY TO YOUR WAITING ROOM

Our work will involve traveling through many doorways. The first doorway you will go through will take you to a place I call the Waiting Room. Anyone who's ever been to a doctor's office or other appointment where you meet with the professional after going through some kind of check-in process should know how to visualize a waiting room. This is not just any room, though, it's *your* Waiting Room, the starting point for every single journey you will take during our time together. You will return to your Waiting Room repeatedly to gain access to whichever area of the

Mindstream you want to go. It all starts from here! All doors originate from your Waiting Room.

When I first started helping clients explore past-life experiences more than twenty years ago and before I actually gave this space a name, I found that I would always go to the same room for some reason each and every time I worked with someone. The room had very specific decorations and looked like a Victorian era parlor. Why? I never knew. I became curious about that and decided to ask my clients to describe the room they saw in our sessions. To my stunned amazement, many described the same exact place I had seen myself. Here's how one client described it:

> I walked inside and there were muted, mauve colors on the walls. To my right, there was a wall that had pictures on it I could not make out. They were hanging on a wall covered with old-fashioned wallpaper. The trim was a dark wood of some kind. In the middle of the room, there was a circular table and some chairs.

When I read this, I couldn't believe it! The description seemed like the exact same room where I had gone each and every time, where I still go to this day. Another client said this:

> It reminds me of a place, say, in the 1800s or so. Like a very old house, neatly decorated, a very nice place, but no place I have ever been before.

Again, I couldn't believe that the client had somehow described the time period so accurately. If I had to guess, I would definitely place the home in the period between the 1800s and 1900s. I've always considered the décor to be Victorian, and since the Victorian era's official dates are 1837 to 1901 during Queen Victoria's reign, the description of the date seemed pretty uncanny.[7] Likewise, the photos the client described on the walls are also there, although sadly, I've never been able to get a good look at them to see who or what is pictured there. Like many details in the Akashic realm or Mindstream, information is revealed on a need-to-know basis. After twenty years, I guess I don't need to know that.

I've also wondered if this room is an actual place I visited or lived during a previous life. The room is so specific, it seems definitely possible. The room is real, and I believe it exists out in the Mindstream. However, I've come to believe over the years that this is not a home I visited during an earthly life. Another question I've asked myself is whether or not I created this room or it already existed and was waiting for me to find it. Again, I have no way to know the answer to that question with a hundred percent certainty even though I know the room, the photos, the round table, and other contents are quite real indeed despite not existing in material reality.

The other concern I struggled with early in my career was the idea that clients saw *my* room, rather than something of their own. I did not want to purposefully project my inner world onto them, so I strengthened my intention to shield the details of my Waiting Room so that clients could have their own inner experiences. Soon after making that shift in my intention, clients began describing all kinds of other rooms and places, some fully furnished, others quite sparsely decorated. All were unique to each person, and the details of décor and style spanned many different eras throughout history.

---

7. Susie Steinbach, "Victorian era," *Encyclopedia Britannica*, October 2019, https://www.britannica.com/event/Victorian-era. Accessed January 2021.

To get the most out of the individualized information in the Mindstream, it's important you create your own special room. For best results, you will go to this room and find yourself doing what I did years ago: returning to that same Waiting Room for every single trip through the Mindstream taken together in this book. That way, the more you practice going to your special Waiting Room (kind of like exercising a muscle or setting up physical sacred space as covered in the last chapter), the stronger your connection and the more vivid your experiences will become.

When clients dealt with trauma, I asked them to create a loving safe place I called the Happy Place, their personal secure room that became the launching pad to help them relieve anxiety. The Waiting Room to access the Akashic Records and Mindstream should also be a safe, supportive space where you feel comfortable; a place you love and enjoy where you feel happy and totally safe and at ease. You may find yourself in a familiar place you've experienced in other meditation programs, or you may go to a different place altogether. Although my Waiting Room has always been an interior space, please don't let my experience influence yours. You may find your Waiting Room is a beautiful outdoor setting—that's perfectly fine! One recent client found herself in a stunning meadow filled with flowers. Others have been in more celestial realms. The setting you call your Waiting Room is yours and yours alone; the manner in which it appears is totally up to you and your higher self. Allow whatever emerges to come through. There's no right or wrong so long as you feel comfortable there. Ready? Let's do this!

Exercise

Sit down in a comfortable chair with your feet on the floor and your hands in your lap. Take a deep, relaxing breath as you close your eyes and begin to imagine a healing beam of pure white light going down through the top of your head. Feel this Astral Light moving through your forehead, your eyes, nose, jaw, and down into your neck. Allow the white light to move through your arms and into your shoulders, your elbows, wrists, hands, and fingertips. Allow this white light to continue traveling through your back, your heart center, and stomach. The light continues to move all the way down to the base of your spine and into your legs, your knees, calves, ankles, and down into the soles of your feet. Feel the energy centers in the soles of the feet opening up and allow the light to travel into the center of the earth. Feel yourself in the middle of heaven and earth. Peaceful and relaxed, the pure white light is strengthening now. Imagine the light becoming more and more powerful, so strong, it begins to pour out of your heart, creating a golden ball of light that surrounds you by about three feet in all directions. Imagine feeling the healing warmth of this golden light as it surrounds you and heals you and know that inside the golden ball, only that which is of your highest good can come through.

Now notice a doorway in front of you. See it, feel it, or just allow yourself to have an inner knowing that it is there. Imagine you can walk through that doorway now, and as you do, you find yourself inside a beautiful room. This is your Waiting Room. Be there now and notice how relaxed you feel here. Look around and see what's there. Notice the good vibrations of this space as you start to explore. Take note of what you see and hear, and how you feel. What does your Waiting Room look like? If you cannot see anything, notice if you can hear any sounds. What are they? How does your Waiting Room feel? Do you see any furniture? Are there any photographs or other decorations? Take your time. Enjoy your exploration.

[pause]

Now imagine you can turn around and move toward the door where you came in. Open that door now and go back out to the place where you started, closing the door behind you. Standing right back where we started, imagine you are still surrounded by that golden ball of light, safe, secure and protected, knowing that within that golden ball of light, only that which is of your highest good can come through. In a moment, when I count back from three, you will return to the room in the present moment, feeling awake, refreshed and better than you did before. Ready? Three, grounded, centered and balanced; two, easily returning to this space at a later time; and one, you're back!

***

How did that go? How did you feel in your Waiting Room? Ideally, you will return to that same room each time we do these exercises, so I hope it's a place you find comforting and relaxing. Remember that you're going to be visiting your Waiting Room a lot, so if you didn't get all the details on your first try, don't worry. I promise you will become quite familiar with this place over time. Go ahead and make any notes in your journal about things you saw there that you might want to recall later on.

SUMMING UP

Learning to access Astral Light and raise your vibrations can have a hugely positive impact on your life. Now that you've succeeded in visiting and establishing your Waiting Room, we will continue to expand our work by introducing you to your spirit guides who can assist you on your path. Later, we will dive into some of the more archetypal examples of the Akashic Records that have taken hold in popular culture, and finally, you'll get to go down the rabbit hole, so to speak, as we access some of the otherworldly and multidimensional aspects of the expansive Mindstream.

These guided processes are kind of like going to a gym—you don't always get exactly what you're looking for the first time you try. For example, you may not be as visual as you'd like to be yet, but keep practicing. Don't worry, and remember to honor your intuitive insights no matter how they come to you. You can continue to explore the processes explained here as many times as needed to get optimal results.

Remember that if you take time to record the journeys as you go, you'll be able to replay them whenever you want to do them. The information that emerges from the Mindstream will change depending on what you're working on at the moment, so that's another reason why you may want to revisit these processes during different times in your life.

Chapter Five

CONNECTING WITH SPIRIT GUIDES

Spirit guides are unseen helpers who communicate with us from beyond the veil. Guides come in many forms: some are angels who have known our souls forever, and others appear in our inner vision as formless beings of pure light. All guides are discarnate, so they can't be seen with the physical eyes. Some of our guides are Ascended Masters such as Buddha, while others are Archangels such as Michael or Raphael; they could also be personal angels or guides who work only with you rather than with humanity at large. Many guides have never inhabited a physical form or human body, and still others are people we've known and loved in the past. For example, I've had many clients who have deceased loved ones or parents come in to act as spirit guides.

Above all, the common denominator all of our guides share is the fact that they are beings who love us unconditionally and who come to assist and protect us in our daily activities. They can provide helpful guidance amidst the chaos of daily life and make us feel as though we are truly never alone and connected with something beyond ourselves.

My personal experience of learning to connect with my guides and receive their loving assistance has been one of the biggest blessings in my life. One of the keys to navigating the Mindstream will be to connect with a trusted guide who will travel with you on all your different inner-dimensional adventures. When I work with any clients, I establish that the guide they meet here is one of the ones who has been with them for all eternity, who loves them fully and completely and knows all there is to know about them and their individual soul. How the guide shows up, or who shows up specifically can differ from person to person, but one thing's for sure—the guide loves you and looks out for you always.

In this chapter, we'll go over everything you need to know about how to meet your guide, what to ask them, and how to build a strong relationship—and even a friendship with them—so you can get the most out of your time in the Akashic Records.

PREPARING TO MEET YOUR SPIRIT GUIDE

Akashic access is available to everyone. The records aren't being watched over by some menacing guardians who hold the keys to the kingdom of the Akashic realm, nor is some outer force preventing you from finding answers to your questions. Still, there's no doubt that guides are incredibly helpful when navigating the information found in the Mindstream. I don't subscribe to the idea that there are certain kinds of guides to guard this or that, primarily due to my own personal experiences from accessing the Akashic Records for so many years.

That said, I do have one specific guide who has consistently shown up for me in my Waiting Room every single time I go there. She looks like a gigantic angel with long hair and wings, like something you would see in a Renaissance painting by Michelangelo. Why her? I have no idea, but whether I'm going to look at my past lives or any other journey, she is always the one who meets me in my Waiting Room.

These days, most of my clients describe a spirit guide who appears in their Waiting Room. For that reason, you will go with your personal guide each time you access the Mindstream. If an angel shows up, that's fine; if it's a being of light, that's also perfect. I am not here to define who shows up for you. Your guide is a being who loves you and will support your journey by holding your hand, answering your questions, and showing you things that will help you gain better understanding of your soul's journey through time. The value of enlisting help from your trusted guide cannot be understated. By refining the information you receive and explaining why your experiences are important, your guide will be a huge part of your soul growth.

Theoretically, it would be awesome if the same guide shows up for you each time you enter your Waiting Room to go into the Mindstream. You could build a relationship with that guide and know that each time you take a journey, you both would be getting to know each other better. Especially since I always have the same guide, I encourage my clients who access these realms often to do their best to see if one single guide can be there for them whenever they work through this material to establish a routine spiritual practice to build upon over time. I recommend setting your intention to keep the same guide each time. That said, you may not always have control over who shows up; if something else happens, always be open to what emerges. For simplicity's sake, having one familiar guide each time is optimal. If you can walk through the same door into the same Waiting Room and meet the same spirit guide, those aspects become the constant part of your journey; the only variables become the healing information and revelations you discover while traveling there.

That said, we are all different and have a unique set of unseen helpers and life lessons we're working on during our journey on earth, so it's definitely possible your guide might change once you start moving through the different doorways and spaces we're going to explore within the Mindstream. If that happens, that's fine; there's no right or wrong. Initially set your intention to meet with someone who will be able to guide you through the Akashic Records. If that guide shows up each time, great; if another shows up, be open. Always follow your unique intuition above all else and know all is well.

HOW GUIDES BEST COMMUNICATE WITH YOU

What's interesting is that our spirit guides use the same means as people do to communicate with us. They try to figure us out so they can best convey their messages. Once we understand how we best receive guidance and acknowledge and honor our unique abilities as covered in the previous chapter, it's easier to open your intuition, receive communication from spirit guides, and ultimately access the Akashic Records. Here are the main ways we receive communication from our guides:

Pictures: Guides love to give you pictures by presenting an image in your mind. When these visual cues appear, they seem to come from out of nowhere, and yet they're solidly fixed in your mind's eye.

Thoughts: Spirit guides may also put a complete thought into your mind, perhaps an idea or some bit of inspiration needed to resolve a conflict or challenge. Perhaps they give you the keys to unlocking a question you had difficulty answering. The thought is always sent in a positive way and can feel like a real breakthrough that emerges from the divine.

Feelings: Some people are more sensitive than others. This is particularly true in the energy healing community. If you're an empath who is incredibly open to feeling what others feel and your guides know that, they may communicate with you through your feelings. Suddenly you have a great feeling about taking a certain action or doing a project, or the feeling may be about a person or a positive resolution to a problem you've struggled to resolve.

Sounds: Some people are more auditory and hear the inner voice. If your guides believe you can hear their loving guidance, you may hear sentences, single words, or even sounds, such as high frequency ringing in the ears. I've experienced my guides speaking to me at times and hear high pitched tones in my ears. The more important the message, the louder the tones will sound. Some may believe they have a case of a medical condition called tinnitus, which is quite real and can be incredibly difficult to handle, but these frequencies from your guides are not constant. They come in periodically to shift your attention inward to hear the guidance and loving direction coming your way, and like energy healing, the sounds can actually open your energy centers and create healing within the body. Another way people can hear sounds and messages from guides is through songs. Sometimes song lyrics perfectly express just the right thing that we need to hear. When a song pops into your mind, especially one that's older or that you don't necessarily hear all the time, rest assured that your guides are trying to tell you something. What do the lyrics say? Pay attention and you'll never know what can happen! Years ago on a trip to India, I started hearing the old 1970s Bob Seger song, "Kathmandu," which has lyrics about going to Kathmandu. After recognizing this song as a sign, I changed my return flight home and stopped by Nepal before returning to the United States. I'm so glad I did! Guides speak to us through songs and music all the time. Recently, one of my energy healing students began getting messages in songs that she delivered to other group members. Each person said the song told them something about things they'd been working on or needed to hear at that moment. It's incredible!

One important note about our guides and their communication methods is that your guides always communicate with you in a loving, positive way. Earlier we discussed prayers and opening to the highest leveled guides and beings of love and light; in the guided journeys you're about to do, you will be able to easily connect with incredibly high leveled guides. As mentioned, your intent is everything. Setting proper intention that you've connected with beings of love and light ensures you always receive positive messaging. Even if you're being warned of some danger or something you should avoid, the feeling behind such a message is always filled with love, light, and your highest good.

ACKNOWLEDGING HELP
AND EXPRESSING GRATITUDE

Once you master how the guides are communicating, you must acknowledge that assistance. How? The best way is to follow the advice if it seems sound. You could also thank your guide or spirit helper for assisting you. Let them know you noticed what they did and say thanks. That way you'll receive more instances of their help and can respond accordingly. I've designed these journeys to acknowledge your guides in a loving and thoughtful way throughout. The more you're grateful for the things you have, the more you will receive. If you thank the guides and let them know you noticed what they provided, more will be on the way to you.

QUESTIONS YOU CAN ASK YOUR GUIDE

Since we're going for a deep relationship that will last for a lifetime, you will want to get to know your guide. And the more you venture into the Mindstream, the better you and your guide will come to understand each other. When we do the guided journey to meet your main guide and subsequent spirit guides, there are several things you may want to know.

What Is Your Name?

Your relationship with your guide should be treated with the same value and respect you would want to experience from a trusted friend, so at some point, most people would want to know their guide's name. There are world traditions in which knowing someone's name means holding a certain degree of power over them, so if you don't feel it's quite time to ask your guide's name yet when first meeting, that's fine. Wait until it seems appropriate. You could also say something such as "How should I address you?" or "What would you like me to call you?"

What Information Will You Share with Me?

I believe that there are different guides who are in charge of different aspects of our soul's journey. As mentioned, I have one clear guide who is always there for the Mindstream journeys written about here. At other times, I've had other guides show themselves to me depending on what I'm working on at any given moment. For that reason, it's always nice to get an idea up front about what information your guide can or will share with you and what their purpose is for being with you.

How Do You Best Communicate with Me?

You may want to know how your guide has communicated with you in the past and how they plan to do so in the future. Did they try pictures, thoughts, or feelings? Did they send you signs or symbols? Numbers, perhaps? There's any number of ways your guides are communicating. Of course in the Mindstream, you'll be initiating the contact each time, but you may want to have an understanding of how the guide has attempted to assist you in the past so you will know how best to receive.

Have You Ever Incarnated on Earth or Are You a Celestial Being Only?

Some guides are benevolent spirit beings who simply assist the living through the veil but have no experience in the ways of living on earth. This might interest you, although it's not necessarily important. Think of details like this as helping you get to know each other better.

Did We Know Each Other in Past Lives?

If the guide has been in physical form, it's possible you may have known them in a previous lifetime. That does happen sometimes but is not always the case. Again, this is simply interesting information to know to help you deepen your connection and friendship.

Ultimately, it is best to go with the flow and allow the information to come in as naturally as possible. Know that if you don't make a connection right away, that's fine too. Keep working until you feel you've received what you need to continue. Let's go now and meet your guide!

Exercise

Close your eyes and immediately notice the familiar beam of pure white light moving through the crown of your head, through your body, and into your feet. This Astral Light easily travels from the top of your head, through your body, and into the core of the earth. You find yourself in the middle of earth and sky, perfectly balanced. Surround yourself with your ball of golden protective light. Know that you invite only that which is of pure love and light and for your highest good to come through. Notice your familiar doorway and open the door now. Step into your Waiting Room, the same room where you went before. Very nice!

Enjoying the energy of this space while feeling safe, relaxed, and at ease, imagine a beautiful spirit guide is floating down in front of you. You can see this guide, feel the guide's presence, hear your guide speaking to you, or just have an inner knowing that your guide is there. Take your time. Feel the unconditional love and high regard your guide has for you. As you experience your guide's energy, what do you notice about their appearance? Take your time to make your observations. What does your guide's energy feel like? How do they sound if they're speaking with you? Have you met this guide before, or is this someone new? Is this the same guide who will help you explore all doorways in the Mindstream? Imagine they can describe through pictures, thoughts, or feelings exactly how they will help you on your journey through the Mindstream. Take your time and ask your guide any other questions you need answers to at this moment.

[pause]

When you're ready, thank your guide for being with you today. Know you will return here soon. Say goodbye for now and imagine your guide is floating away. Walk through the door again and close it behind you. When I count back from three, you will return to waking consciousness. Ready? Three, feeling relaxed and at ease; two, surrounded by healing light, knowing you're safe in all activities; and one, you're back!

***

What information did your guide share with you today? What did your guide look like, or did you only feel their presence? Remember not to be disappointed if you didn't see much yet. That can definitely expand over time. As mentioned, for many years, I only ever had feelings emerge, but saw very little. If you could only feel your guide, that's fine! Over time, you may start to open up visually, but regardless of whether you see, hear, or feel your guide, the information is still valuable and valid. I wish we were sitting here together because I would love to hear all about what you experienced and how your guide will be helping you in the Mindstream. Take your journal out and write down anything important so you will remember that information later. I hope getting to your Waiting Room has become easier now. Know it's going to become even more familiar to you as we move forward.

MEETING GUIDES IN HIGHER DIMENSIONS

I've been asked numerous times over the years to help students meet and hear insights from their spirit guides. Next, you will take a fun journey that will give you your first trip into some of the higher dimensional realms where information from the Akashic Records can be obtained. Although our goal for working in the Mindstream is to meet with one guide who is in charge of helping you, in reality we all have many different kinds of spirit guides and helpers who assist us with different aspects of our soul journey. Some have been in physical form in the past, while others are more celestial and may appear only as light beings.

In this next exercise, you will go back into your Waiting Room where you will hopefully meet with your main guide met in the last exercise. From there, you will have a chance to travel out into the Mindstream to encounter some of your other special guides who work behind the scenes to help your soul navigate the fascinating waters of daily life. You will be traveling up into a very high frequency dimension to make contact with this group of advisors and ascend beyond the earth realm to a space where you will be met by numerous beings of light who will help you raise your frequency. This process is a longtime favorite of many of my clients, and I can't wait to share this with you! Ready? Let's begin!

Exercise

Sit down in a comfortable chair. Breathe in through your nose, and exhale out your mouth. Establish your connection to Astral

Light; allow that light to move through the top of your head, travel through your body, and exit through the soles of your feet, connecting you now with the core of the earth. The light moves through your heart center and creates your protective shield of golden light that surrounds your entire body. Know that within this protective golden light that only that which is of your highest good can come through. Notice the door to your Waiting Room. Open the door and step inside. Notice that your loving guide is floating down to join you. You may notice this is the same guide you met with earlier. Take a moment to set your intention and discuss the journey you'd like to take today. Let your guide know that you would like to travel into a space in a higher dimension where you will be able to meet with some of your other high leveled guides, helpers, and beings of love and light who currently assist you on your path.

Notice across the room, there's an elevator. Go with your guide and walk or float inside the elevator. As you do so, you notice the buttons. You're currently on the floor representing the third dimension and you want to go all the way up to the highest dimension possible, the dimension your guide feels is for your highest good at this time. Go ahead now and press the button for one of the higher dimensions. The elevator doors are closing and you begin to feel the elevator moving up, up, up, higher and higher. Notice that the higher up the elevator goes, the more relaxed you feel as you find yourself expanding into a higher state of awareness. In a moment, when I count to three, you will arrive at the floor and dimension that is most for your highest good. Ready? One, two, and three, you're there. The elevator doors are opening and you can be there now. Imagine you can ask your guide for clarification. What dimension is this? Observe the first thought that floats into your mind.

Follow your guide; the two of you will walk or float out of the elevator. Notice you're inside a large room filled with high frequency light. Several beings of pure love and light are there to meet you today. As you step further into this room, notice how easy it is to feel the incredible unconditional love that these beings have for you. Bask in the high vibrations of this room as the beings welcome you. Very good!

Notice at the other side of the room, there's a doorway there. Imagine you can follow your main spirit and the two of you can walk or float through the crowd of light beings toward that door on the other side of the room. When you're ready, put your hand on the doorknob and open the door. Do that now and you and your guide find yourself walking or floating inside another high frequency room where there are more guides there to help you and relay important personal information. Your main guide shows you a velvet curtain. When you walk beyond that curtain, you will receive answers to your questions. When you're ready, pull the velvet curtain back and step inside. Very good! Now go ahead and receive what you need to know at this time. See what you need to see, hear what you need to hear, and notice how you feel. Take your time and ask any questions until you feel clear about this guidance. What are these guides here to help you with? How will this information add value to your current life journey? Receive other impressions now through pictures, thoughts and feelings.

[pause]

Now, thank these light beings for the information they've shared today. Go ahead and pull the velvet curtain back, reconnect with your main spirit guide, and walk through the outer room into the first room with the other beings of light. Thank them all for participating in your journey today. Say goodbye for now and know you can return here later to receive further information.

Notice the elevator. You and your main guide can now walk or float up to that elevator, reach out, and push the down button and watch the doors open in front of you. You and your personal guide will now step inside and notice the panel with the buttons. You're all the way up in a higher dimension, and in just a moment you will go all the way back down to the third dimension. Push the button for the third dimension. The doors close and you begin to feel the elevator going down, down, down, back toward earth and the third dimension. In a moment, when I count to three, you will arrive back where you started. One, two, and three, you're back!

The elevator doors open and you and your guide are now inside your Waiting Room where you began your journey. Take a moment to ask your personal guide any important questions about what happened today. How can these other guides help you on the spiritual path? What is their purpose compared to your main guide? Take your time to receive clarity.

[pause]

When you're ready, thank your guide for helping today. Walk or float back through the door where we started. Close the door to the Waiting Room and step out to your starting point. Still surrounded by your golden healing light, safe and protected, in a moment, when I count back from five, you will return and feel awake, refreshed, and better than you felt before. Ready? Five, grounded, centered and balanced in the third dimension and waking reality; four, processing this information and energy in your dreams tonight so that by tomorrow morning you will be fully integrated into this new awareness; three, driving and being safe in all activities; two, returning to your physical body; one, and you're back.

***

How did you do with that journey? What dimension did you visit today? I did not specify which dimension you should visit on purpose so you could go wherever was most for your highest good. I truly believe we only go where we're meant to be. Who did you meet? Why was the encounter so important? You may also want to reconnect with these higher dimensions periodically depending what you're working on. As always, I encourage you to make a few notes about your journey.

MEETING YOUR OTHERWORLDLY GUIDES

Another client favorite is our next journey where you'll travel into a mystical land and connect with special guides—fairies, unicorns, and the like, who will assist you connecting to a feeling of abundance. These will likely be different guides than the ones you've already met. They're a special set you can call on to assist with creating a feeling of profound happiness who will help you tap into your unlimited nature.

Exercise

Sit in your comfortable place and relax. Breathe. Connect with Astral Light and invite that light to move through the top of your head, your forehead, eyes, nose, mouth, neck, shoulders, and move into your arms, hands and fingers, into your neck, heart, stomach, moving to the base of your spine and into your legs, knees, and into your feet. Allow the Astral Light to become a waterfall that pours through you carrying tensions and concerns out the soles of your feet. Connect with the earth center. As you do, the Astral Light becomes so overpowering; it pours out of your heart center, creating a bright green ball of light that surrounds you and opens you to your heart's desire, abundance, and prosperity.

Floating in this green healing light ball, imagine you can feel the healing energies of that light as you walk through the familiar door and go into your Waiting Room. Meet your guide and say hello. State your intention for today by telling your guide that you would like to meet other guides to help you with abundance. Follow your guide to a door on the other side of your Waiting Room. Your guide is opening that door now. Go through the door with your guide and find yourself standing in front of a crystal staircase that spirals up into the clouds.

Still surrounded by your healing green ball of light, follow your guide and begin walking up the steps of the crystal staircase. Ready? One, two, three, four, five, becoming more relaxed with each step; six, seven, climbing the stairs going higher and higher; and eight. You're there. Be there now. Find yourself in a totally different world. As you look around, you realize this is the most beautiful place you've ever seen, a magical land of unlimited possibilities. Notice the colors, flowers, sky, trees, and grass.

Notice interesting creatures begin to emerge. You may see a unicorn galloping in front of you, or notice animals, fairies, sprites and other benevolent spirits. Notice what you notice and feel the loving vibrations of every being you encounter. Know that these loving energies are your special guides. Imagine these guides are welcoming you and leading you to a little footbridge over a stream. In a moment, you and your main guide will cross this bridge and go with these loving creatures. And before we cross the bridge, just know that you are crossing over into something very real. You're going to a place where you can create, be all you've ever wanted to be, and have all you've ever wanted to have. You're moving into a place of complete happiness and freedom. Ready? Go ahead and cross over that bridge now. As you do, feel yourself expanding more and more, and imagine you can expand that green ball of light to encompass that whole area. Become one with everything you see.

Notice the trees. See now that these are money trees! The wind is picking up and the money is falling, just falling everywhere! Because the money represents life force, notice the money's just growing on the trees because you have more than enough. You have everything you ever need. Allow yourself to totally connect with the money falling off the trees as if you are one and the same, peaceful, relaxed and prosperous. Notice a footpath in front of you. Walk down the path as the money continues to sprinkle down on you. Imagine you can bathe in this money bath.

Still walking through this beautiful forest, up ahead you see a big rock. Stand by the rock and notice several beings approaching you now. These are your guides. Your guides welcome you into this creative space of your greatest abundance. Say hello and greet each of them. Notice what you notice about their appearance and if you feel so guided, ask their names or any other questions.

[pause]

Thank them for helping you today. When you're ready, turn and go back, feeling empowered and energized. Go back toward the footbridge, continuing to be showered by the rainfall of money, the rain of blessings and abundance. Walk over the footbridge now and notice the river just flowing gently, flowing with the greatest of ease, just as abundance now flows effortlessly for you. You are a part of the flow, easily creating all you truly desire, recognizing yourself as an infinite being capable of anything and everything, part of the flow of abundance in the universe. Good job!

Walk toward the crystal staircase and begin going down the eight steps toward your Waiting Room. Ready? Eight, peaceful and relaxed; seven, six, five, four, three, two, one, and you're back. Walk through the door to your Waiting Room. Thank your guide and walk once more through the door you arrived, and be back where you started. Still surrounded by a green healing light, you continue to carry this green ball of light with you, knowing that green light represents abundance, prosperity, and everything that is for your highest good. When I count back from three, you will return, feeling better than ever before. Three, grounded, centered and balanced; two, processing this new energy and abundant vibration in your dreams and integrating fully by tomorrow; and one, you're back!

***

How do you feel? I hope you enjoyed that magical journey. What ideas did your new guides share with you? Use this process anytime you want another fun way to connect with your guides.

SUMMING UP

I hope you enjoyed meeting your main spirit guide who will be working with you throughout your exploration of the Mindstream. Take time to reflect also on all the information received from the many loving beings who assist you in other worlds and dimensions. There is much to gain from such reflection. Remember, you can journey into these spaces however many times you need to get clarity. Know that you will be getting to know your main guide very well as we continue through the book, and over time, your guide will become a trusted friend.

Chapter Six

TRADITIONAL AKASHIC ARCHETYPES

Now that you've established a solid starting point via your Waiting Room and have met and worked with your special guide, we're going to begin moving through several areas within the Mindstream that will allow you to access your Akashic Records. First, I will show you some of the more common ways to access the Akashic Records that are in alignment with some of the wider held archetypes of the records and what you can find there. I hope these fun processes yield helpful information for you.

AKASHIC LIBRARY

This first exercise is the most traditional means I know of to access the Akashic Records. Earlier we discussed the idea that the Akashic Records are a multidimensional space, yet in order to go where you need to go, you must create some common places to access this nonphysical reality. When people think of records (and especially the Akashic Records), they often envision a library, so in this journey, you will visit an otherworldly library and receive the information that you most want or need to know from books in the library. Before you begin, decide in advance what you want to find there or if you'd just like to receive whatever serves your highest good. In the journey, you will be asked per usual to share your specific intention with your guide. If you don't have that firmly in your mind yet, take time to consider one and then continue whenever you are prepared. Assuming you know what you'd like to ask about, let's do this!

Exercise

Sit in a comfortable chair with your feet flat on the floor and your hands in your lap. Close your eyes. Relax. Take a deep, healing breath in through your nose. Connect with the Astral Light and imagine that pure white light moving down through the top of your head. Feel the light travel into your head, your neck and shoulders, into your arms, wrists, hands, and fingertips. Allow the Astral Light to move down through your heart, into your stomach. Fill your lungs with pure white light as you breathe in love, peace, and joy. Exhale. Very good.

Imagine that with every breath you take, you're becoming more and more relaxed. Allow that light to continue through your heart, moving down, down, down to the base of your spine, moving into your legs—your thighs, knees, ankles and all the way down through the soles of your feet. Connect to the earth center and feel the light pouring through you carrying away any tensions and concerns and allowing those to move down, down, down into the earth where they are transformed into a beautiful healing light that you're sending to the earth right now. Acknowledge that you are now in the perfect center between heaven and earth.

Allow this light to become stronger and stronger as it pours through you from head to toe. Notice you're connected from head to toe in the middle of this pure white field of light. Feel the light pouring out of your heart center creating a beautiful, golden ball of light that surrounds you by about three feet in all directions. Feel yourself floating inside this golden protective light. Know that within this light that only that which is of your highest good can come through. Very nice!

Imagine noticing the doorway to your Waiting Room in front of you. See the door, feel the door, or just know that door is there. In a moment when I count back from three, you're going to open that door and step inside your Waiting Room. Ready? Three, two, one, open the door now.

Walk or float through the door and notice you feel totally at ease and relaxed. Your guide floats down from above and greets you. Go ahead now and state your intention for today by telling your guide exactly what information you want to retrieve from the Akashic Library and Hall of Records today. If have any questions you need to ask your guide before you begin, go ahead and do that now, or allow your guide to clarify anything for you.

[pause]

Nice job! Feel the loving energy of your guide and this beautiful energy inside your Waiting Room. As you do, you notice on the other side of the room, there's a doorway there. Take your guide by the hand and walk or float up to that door now. Open the door and imagine you're looking into a tunnel of light. Notice how compelling and peaceful this light feels and looks. In a moment, when I count to three, you will go through this tunnel of light toward the Akashic Library and the Hall of Records. Ready? One, two, and three, float into that light now.

Imagine you're floating very quickly now, faster and faster, noticing that the more you float, the more relaxed you feel. In a moment, when I count to three, you will arrive at your destination.

Ready? One, two, and three—you're out of the tunnel of light and have landed inside a vast room. Still holding your guide's hand, step out of the tunnel now, and as you do, you'll notice you're on the ground floor of a stunning building. Take a look around. Notice what you notice. See what you see, feel what you feel, and hear any sounds. As you do, notice that you feel totally relaxed and at ease in this space. You're there with your guide and remember that you are still surrounded by your golden ball of light that protects you. You understand that within the light, only that which is of your highest good can come through.

Imagine you've arrived at the main library for the Hall of Records. You can walk or float up to a main entrance. There may be an information desk or you may notice some kind of signage showing what information is located on every floor of this vast structure. Notice these items are arranged according to your interests. You can either see this in writing, have your guide tell you what's there or allow yourself to have an inner knowing. Go ahead now and recall your intention you set for your journey today. What did you want to know about? Notice that inside this library, any subject you can think of is available, including the one you're asking about.

Locate the floor of this library where your subject can be found. When you do, you and your loving guide begin walking or floating through the building toward an elevator. Step up to that elevator now and imagine the doors open. You and your guide are stepping inside. See the light panel and notice all the buttons. Imagine they're labeled by subject matter. Go ahead now and push the button corresponding to the floor you'd like to visit today. As you push that button now, you notice the doors are closing and you and your guide are moving up, up, up, faster and faster. Notice that the higher up you go, the more relaxed you feel as you move toward the floor you want to visit today. On the count of three, you will arrive to the correct floor. Ready? One, two, and three. You're there! Be there now.

The doors open and you and your guide walk or float out to the floor where the items are located. Step out of the elevator. Directly in front of you is a giant book that contains the information you seek. Go with your guide as the two of you walk or float closer to that book. You may notice if it's already opened to a page, or if not, go ahead now and open the book to a page that that will best address your intentions. Read that page now. Notice what you notice. Feel what you feel. See what you see. If you need to flip through several pages, imagine your guide can help you do that now. Your guide can also tell you what's there if needed. Take your time and imagine you can receive all that is for your Highest Good at this moment in time that relates to what you wanted to know today.

[**pause**]

Very good! Imagine now that your guide closes the book. Say a prayer of thanks for the transformational information you've received today. When you're ready, turn and walk back to the elevator. Open the doors and imagine you and your guide can walk or float into the elevator. Push the ground button and begin moving down, down, down, back toward the lobby of the building. Move across that space and feel yourself moving quickly now, through the tunnel of light. When I count to three, you will be back in your Waiting Room. Ready? One, two and three. Be there now! Thank your special guide again for helping you today. Notice also that you're still surrounded by your golden healing light, safe, secure, protected. You know that within the golden light, only that which is of your highest good can come through.

Take a few moments to ask your guide important questions about the information you received in the Akashic Records library. Why is that information relevant to you at this moment in your soul's history? How will you use the information in your current life? What lessons will you learn or achievements do you hope to make now that you've accessed this information? Take your time and ask for further clarity from your guide.

[pause]

When you're ready, thank your guide again and turn and go out the Waiting Room door, back to the place where you first started your journey today. Be there now. In a moment, when I count back from five, you will return. Five, grounded, centered and balanced; four, processing all the energy and information received in your dreams tonight so that by tomorrow morning you will be fully integrated into this new awareness; three, driving safely and being safe in all activities; two, grounded, centered, and balanced; and one, you're back!

***

How did you do? Definitely write down what you experienced in the library. What did the book say? How did your guide describe the helpfulness and timeliness of this information? Make any other notes and know that your future self is really going to thank you for taking the time to record this information that will hopefully help you on your soul's path through your current lifetime.

COSMIC COMPUTER

Another common archetype in the discussion about Akashic Records is the idea that our modern internet and worldwide web are physically manifested aspects of everything that exists in the Akashic Records, as if we humans are just scrambling as fast as we can to grab all we can from the ethers and put those ideas and concepts down to store them in one place. This next journey is for the tech savvy folks who would like to visit a cosmic computer lab to receive answers to life's mysteries.

Exercise

Set your intention for what you want to know. Sit in your space, relax, and surround yourself with golden light. Within your golden light, only that which is of the highest love and light can come through. Now go into your Waiting Room like you did before. Meet your guide and let them know that today, you'd like to see your records on a computer relating to whatever you've intended to discover. Notice a door on the other side of the room and follow your guide into a new area filled with tons of computers. Take a look around. Notice what you notice. Know that here you are safe, secure, and totally protected. Follow your guide through the lab up to a computer and take a seat. Use the computer and imagine you can easily open a document or a website that tells all about what you most want to know. Take your time to gather all the information you need. If necessary, your guide can read this information to you, or you can easily have an inner knowing about what's there.

[pause]

When you're ready, get up and go with your guide back into your Waiting Room. Say thank you and walk back to where you began. Still surrounded by your golden ball of light, when I count back from three, you will return. Ready? Three, grounded, centered and balanced; two, processing what you learned in your dreams tonight and becoming totally clear by morning; and one, you're back!

***

How did you enjoy your computer? Did you discover a document, a website, or both? Did you like the technology rather than the books? Both can be fun and yield different results, depending on what you most need to know.

SPHINX JOURNEY

Years ago during a meditation, I accidentally found myself in an alternative dimension traveling underneath the paw of the Great Sphinx of Giza in Egypt. I saw myself floating up to the Sphinx, and as I faced it, I went under the paw to my left—the Sphinx's' *right paw* that Edgar Cayce referred to in his prophecy. I wish I could recall more details of how and why this happened, but I assume my many years of study and fascination with Cayce's life had a profound influence on me. In this next journey, you'll go on a similar trip to experience the Akashic Records from an ancient hall located under the right paw of the Sphinx. Be sure to decide on your intention before you go.

Exercise

Sit in a comfortable space where you feel nurtured and supported. Close your eyes and begin to relax. Breathe in love and light and peace, and exhale any tensions. Connect to the Astral Light. Allow the beautiful beam of light to pour through you from head to toe, connecting you with the earth and sky. Feel the Astral Light surrounding you by about three feet in all directions. Imagine feeling yourself bathed in a golden ball of healing light and know that within this loving light, only that which is of your highest good can ever come through.

Notice the familiar doorway in front of you. Walk or float into your Waiting Room. Notice what you notice, hear what you hear, see what you see, and feel the loving vibrations of this special place as your lovely spirit guide joins you. This may be the same guide you've worked with before or it could be someone new. Say hello and feel the unconditional love and high regard the guide has for you. Imagine your guide will assist you today as you travel into the Akashic Records in Egypt. Take a moment and ask your guide anything you'd like and tell your guide what information you would like to receive from the Akashic Records today.

[**pause**]

When you're ready, imagine noticing a doorway on the other side of this room. Go with your guide and walk or float over to that door now. In a moment, when I count to three, you will open the door and find yourself in the Egyptian desert. Ready? One, two, and three—opening the door now. Walk or float with your guide out into the desert. Be there now. Imagine yourself standing in the sand. Up ahead, you notice the Giza Plateau and the Sphinx. When I count to three, you and your guide will float over to the area near the pyramids and you will find yourself near the Sphinx. Ready? One, two, and three—you're there, standing in front of the Sphinx. Imagine you can walk or float closer. Notice now there's a doorway in the right paw. Open the door and walk or float into the paw of the Sphinx. Be there now, standing inside the Sphinx. Feeling peaceful, safe, and relaxed, you can be there now with your loving guide inside the Sphinx. Walk into the space and notice what you notice, see what you see, hear what you hear and imagine you feel totally at ease as you explore. You're still surrounded by a healing golden light and just know that within this light, only that which is of your highest good can come through.

Up ahead of you, imagine you notice a slide like something you may have played on when you were a child. Imagine you're walking toward the top of this inviting slide that leads downward. The slide feels safe and secure and it looks fun. Go to the slide and imagine you and your loving guide can get on that slide. Go ahead now and feel yourself sliding down the slide with your guide, having so much fun! The feeling is breathtaking! You notice that the further down you slide, the more relaxed you feel. So relaxed, so joyful and playful, having so much fun. You are moving very quickly now as you and your guide slide down, down, down into the area underneath the Sphinx. Going down, down, down, you're laughing and having so much fun as you slide down, down, down, under the desert floor into the area under the Sphinx. Down, down, down to the cavern deep beneath the Sphinx. In a moment when I count to three, you and your guide will arrive to a chamber underneath the Sphinx. Ready? One, sliding down, down, down; two, further and further and further; and three, you're there. Be there now on the ground level.

Imagine you can be there now, inside the space. You notice that you're inside a room with thick earthen walls. Step off the slide, take your guide by the hand, and begin to explore. Notice what's there. You may find staircases there that take you even further down, or not. Imagine you can continue to move through this area for the next several moments, going as deep into the earth as you can possibly go. Going down, down, down, and walking around this area, you may notice symbols or hieroglyphs. Notice what you notice as you continue moving through these tunnels and caverns where you feel safe, secure, and really excited about this journey.

In a moment when I count to three, you will arrive at the lowest level that you can possibly go. One, going down into the cavern; two, so relaxed; and three, you're there. Find yourself inside an expansive room. Look around, notice what you see. You may see papyrus or other documents. You may find books there.

Imagine as you and your guide are taking in this expansive energy of all that's offered here, you can reaffirm your intention. What would you like to know or look up? Bring that question into your awareness, and once again share that with your guide. Very good. Now imagine that as you walk or float through this vast collection of antiquity, you notice the area is filled with books, objects, artifacts and other items. Notice what you notice, feel what you feel, and see what you see. Allow your guide to give you a tour of this hall filled with records, and know that your guide is leading you toward the information you most need to access at this time in your soul history.

[pause]

Your guide is pointing ahead to a table, upon which some kind of document is resting. The document is for you. It may or may not be a book; it may be a scroll, papyrus, or some other kind of document. As you get closer to that document, you know for sure that this document is for you. Allow your guide to remain by your side as you approach that document. Take your time to look over the text. Notice what it says and what information emerges. You can either read it yourself, or if it's in a language you cannot comprehend, imagine your guide can tell you about the contents or simply have an inner knowing. Do that now. Take a moment to review the information. Allow yourself to come to full understanding of your document.

[**pause**]

As you review the material in this sacred space, imagine you can ask why these insights emerged. What does this document tell you about your soul's journey through time? Does the document provide clues about your past lives? What does it reveal about your soul purpose? How will you make use of this information in your current lifetime? How will you apply this new knowledge as you move forward on your current life path? What areas of your life must now change and evolve due to this new information? Take your time. Allow this insight to settle into your mind and your guide to assist you in uncovering any important details.

[**pause**]

Finish your inspection of the document and put the object back where you found it or allow your guide to return it where it belongs for safekeeping. Thank your guide for bringing you here today and for assisting you. Imagine you can take all the energy and awareness from this experience that you will need. When you're ready, imagine you can turn around, take your guide by the hand, and move through this collection, the room and tunnel system, and the area under the Sphinx. You arrive at something that looks like a modern-day elevator. Walk or float over to that elevator. Imagine when I count to three, that elevator is going to open. One, two, and three, it's opening now. Follow your guide into the elevator and push the "up" button. The doors are closing, and you're going up, up, up, up, up, higher and higher and higher and higher, bringing the energy and awareness with you. And on the count of three, the elevator will stop. One, two, and three, it's stopped. The doors are opening and you're able to go with your guide and step out of the elevator. You find yourself back inside your Waiting Room where you started. Be back now.

Take a moment to thank your guide again. Feel the unconditional love your guide has for you. Take all of this energy and awareness with you now as you go back toward the door you first came in, walk through the door, closing the door behind you. You're back where you started still surrounded by a loving, healing, golden ball of light. In a moment when I count back from five, you will return feeling awake, refreshed, and better than you felt before. Ready? Five, you're grounded, centered and balanced; four, continuing to process this information in your dreams tonight so that by tomorrow morning you will be fully integrated into this new energy and awareness; three, driving safely and being safe in every activity; two, grounded, centered, and balanced; and one, you're back!

***

What did you think of that journey? Were you able to get the information you wanted? What surprised you? Be sure to capture any thoughts or insights you received.

AKASHIC CAVE OF SECRETS

Next up, we will access the Akashic Records by having you journey like Indiana Jones into an archaeological site where you can access every hidden detail and treasure of your soul. This is a fun process I hope you will enjoy.

Exercise

Sit in your comfortable space and close your eyes. Draw the Astral Light down from the universe and allow that light to move through your head, limbs, torso, and out the soles of your feet. Feel the light pulling into the earth center and simultaneously expand up to the heavens. Relax and breathe. Feel the light establishing your familiar golden ball of protective light around you and know that within the embrace of the Astral Light, you are safe and totally secure now and always. Notice the doorway to your Waiting Room in front of you. Open that door now and step inside. Your guide is there. Greet your guide and tell them what information you would like to know today. Take a moment and set your intentions.

[pause]

Very good! When you're ready, take your guide by the hand and walk or float over to a door that's just off of your Waiting Room. Open that door and the two of you will find yourselves outside in a mountainous region. Accompanied by your guide, the two of you will walk, float, or even hike through this terrain. Notice what you notice, feel what you feel, hear what you hear, and see what you see. All the while, know you are safe and secure and that you experience this space as fun and exciting. In a moment, when I count to three, you and your guide will find yourselves next to a cave in the side of a mountain. Ready? One, floating through the region; two, feeling safe and excited about the adventure you're about to have; and three, you're there. Be there now, standing next to the opening of a cave. Safe and secure, go with your guide into this cave. Take a look around and imagine as you move into this space, you notice incredible artifacts and writings that have to do with your soul's journey. Up ahead, the walls of the cave become illuminated and you see writing on the rock with clues about the information you are seeking. Imagine you can read that writing, or ask your guide for clarification about the meaning of this message. Take your time. Notice what you notice.

[pause]

When you're finished, imagine noticing more artifacts inside this cave including a written document of some kind. It may be writing on stones, tablets, scrolls, or in another form. Gaze at this information and imagine you can receive even more knowledge about your soul. As you do, know your guide is with you and can clarify anything you need to know more about. Take your time to receive all you need in this ancient space.

[pause]

When you're ready, take your guide's hand and walk or float out of the cave. Be back outside in the mountainous region and by the time I count to three, you will arrive back to the door of your Waiting Room. Ready? One, floating back; two, almost there; and three, you've arrived. Open the door and enter your Waiting Room, closing the door behind you. Take your time to thank your guide and receive any further clarification or insights about the information you received from this special cave.

[**pause**]

Now turn and walk to the door you first entered and go back out to where you started. Close the door and be there now. Still surrounded by golden light, in a moment, when I count back from three, you will return. Three, processing the information you receive in your dreams so that by tomorrow you will be fully integrated into this new energy; two, feeling awake and refreshed and able to go about safely doing all activities; one, you're back!

***

How did you enjoy your adventures in the Akashic cave? I always find it fun to give an adventurous tone to journey work; it helps you uncover the hidden mysteries of your soul.

HALL OF RECORDS

In the spirit of the concept that the Akashic Records are often considered to be inside some great hall, this next journey is a fun way to get in touch with that archetype.

Exercise

Sit and breathe. Close your eyes. Bring your intentions for this journey into your mind. Draw upon the Astral Light to cleanse your energy field as you shield yourself with your golden ball of light. Whenever you're ready, walk through the door into your Waiting Room and meet your guide. Let your guide know what your intention is today and that you'd like to visit the Hall of Records.

[**pause**]

When you're both ready, take your guide's hand and notice a doorway. Walk or float up to the door and open it. As you do, you notice this is a huge room filled with file cabinets and records. Notice those now. Notice also the décor—is the room modern or ancient? What time period does it appear to be from? Go with your guide and walk inside this vast storehouse and imagine your guide can lead you down the many aisles to a file cabinet that is meant for you.

When I count to three, you will arrive to the appropriate cabinet. Ready? One, you're walking through the hall; two, moving past all the records; and three, arriving to the correct place now. Allow your guide to open the file cabinet and pull out a file. Your guide hands the file to you now. Open it and read what's there, or if your guide can help interpret the information for you, allow them to do so. Take your time to receive whatever you need and ask your guide for any clarification.

[pause]

When you're done viewing the documents, hand them over and allow your guide to put them away. Take their hand and quickly float back to the door you first entered. On the count of three, you will arrive at that door. One, two, and three, you're there. Open the door and return to your Waiting Room. Close that door behind you. Thank your guide and ask about any other details you need. Imagine it's easy to receive this information.

When you're ready, walk back to the door you first entered and go back to where you started, closing the door to your Waiting Room behind you. Surrounded by golden light that you will keep with you always, you know that when I count back from three, you will return to waking consciousness, filled with insights from your experience today. Three, grounded and balanced; two, processing the details in your dreams; and one, coming back.

***

What did you think of the Hall of Records? How did it appear? What items were you able to access today? Were you able to receive different material than what you saw in the other Akashic library? Wonderful work!

SUMMING UP

Wow, you did it! You've managed to go through some of the most common ways that take you into the Akashic Records. I hope you had successful journeys with at least one of these methods. Remember that through consistent practice, more information emerges over time. You're bound to find one method you like better than others or that seems easier to tune into. Which one worked the best? Which one did you enjoy the most? I'd say go with the one you like the best and stick with what's easy. Life should be fun, so above all have fun exploring!

Chapter Seven

PSYCHIC PROTECTION AND PRESENT LIFE HEALING

More often than not, I cannot begin a past-life regression without first addressing painful issues in my client's present lifetime. When you think about it, most of us don't pursue any kind of self-analysis when things are going great. Most of my clients show up when something from their present lifetime is awry—they're having relationship troubles, financial difficulties, or are suffering from grief or loss of some kind. The only reason to pursue a regression in the first place is to make our current life experience more peaceful. That's why it's so important that before we ever go into the multiple areas of the Akashic Records to discover things about ourselves from the past, we must first look at our present lifetime.

You may not have considered the fact that the Akashic Records could be used to help out with current situations, but I assure you the records are quite helpful for this purpose. All time is now, so the present is occurring alongside our past and future. The Mindstream has several doorways you can open to have meaningful and transformational encounters with individuals who need your attention and energy from your current lifetime. I'm a firm believer in the idea that current life healing must be addressed first in order to gain greater transformations in other areas of the vast storehouse of information accessible in the records.

Another challenge many of my clients face is learning to protect their energy and keep personal space clear of what I call unwanted influences. These days, there are many books and discussions about highly sensitive people and empaths who unwittingly pick up energy from others, both good and bad. Raising your conscious awareness of how you feel in any given moment is something that will make a drastic improvement in your life. To access these energy field strengthening exercises, you will journey into the Akashic realm and the Mindstream, where you can learn to become more aware of your own energy.

This chapter will take you through some of the most powerfully transformational journeys I've used to help my clients find healing from present life difficulties. First, we will establish a peaceful space where you can work, then we will move on to include exercises for psychic shielding and protection, and finally we'll address challenges with specific people and situations you may be facing in daily life.

BEAUTIFUL PLACE IN NATURE

In this peaceful journey, you will travel into the Akashic Mindstream where you will experience a gorgeous outside environment where your soul can rest and heal. It's an exercise I've used frequently through the years to assist clients struggling with trauma or anxiety. These days, we can all benefit from a special place in beautiful surroundings where our soul can be still and quiet. Obviously going outside in a real natural setting is best, but when that isn't possible or if you need a quick pick-me-up before dealing with a stressful situation, this process can help. To get there, you will go through your doorway used to access the Akashic Records and you'll go into the Mindstream. This area will help you to establish a calm state of mind and find a sense of peace within yourself.

Exercise

Begin in your comfortable space. Close your eyes and draw down the Astral Light through your head and body and allow it to travel to your feet, connecting you with earth and sky. Surround yourself by golden light and walk through the door and go into your Waiting Room, where your loving guide is waiting for you.

As you look around your Waiting Room, you notice there is another doorway at the other side of the room. Go over and open that door. As you do, you notice you and your guide are about to step outside into a beautiful place in nature. Go ahead now and walk or float outside. Look up at the sky. Notice if it's a sunny or cloudy day.

Do you hear any birds or see any animals around? Are there any mountains? Are there any bodies of water? If so, what kind? Notice what you notice, feel what you feel, and allow yourself to bask in the relaxing energy of this beautiful place. As you experience this energy, you feel completely safe and relaxed, peaceful and at ease.

As you begin to notice your surroundings, imagine that you see a tree off in the distance. Go with your guide now and walk or float toward the tree. What kind of a tree is it? Notice it and feel yourself drawn to its energy. As you approach the tree, imagine you can put your arms around it. Feel the amazing energy and allow the tree to share its strength with you. Feel that energy moving in through every cell of your being from the top of your head to the tips of your toes. Very good. Now imagine you can release the tree and turn around. Go ahead and put your back against your tree. Press your spine into the trunk and feel the powerful energy surging through you, strengthening and relaxing you. Good job.

Allow any stresses from your daily life to now to move through your body and into the trunk of this tree. Know that the tree is more than happy to assist you in this way, and any stressful energy you transfer to your tree will be immediately transformed into a loving high frequency energy that your tree will love. Feel the tension releasing as this unwanted energy is moving into the tree trunk. Imagine the tree is benefitting from this energy, as if your tension becomes a fertilizer with beneficial and welcomed nutrients for the tree. Notice how the tree transforms that energy and reciprocates by sending you love and light. Allow that love and light to fill in all the spaces previously occupied by the tension you released. Take your time. Go through every single cell of your being, starting from the tips of your toes, moving into your feet, your legs, your spine and torso, your heart center, your neck, shoulders, arms, and hands, and your entire head. Feel yourself filling with deep peace as this light moves through you. Take your time and if you need more assistance, know that your guide is also there to help you.

[pause]

When you're ready, pull away from the tree trunk and begin to walk or float with your guide back through the door where you came in. Find yourself back inside your Waiting Room. Close the door behind you and know you can return here at any time when you need to experience greater peace and relaxation. Thank your guide for accompanying you today. When you're ready, turn and walk out the door of your Waiting Room. Go back to the space where you first began your journey. In a moment when I count back from three, you will return feeling more relaxed and at ease than ever before. Three, grounded, centered, and balanced; two, you're filled with love and peace; and one, you're back!

***

How did that go? What did your natural setting look like? Did you have any feelings emerge? What kind of tree did you find there? Is it a space you've seen before in the real world or someplace new to you? I hope you will turn to this exercise any time you need to relieve stress. Coming up, you will return to your place in nature to begin some of the other journeys we will take, so this is a good starting point and is a great way to start or end your day by simply being and relaxing.

PSYCHIC PROTECTION IN THE AKASHIC RECORDS AND MINDSTREAM

Throughout the book we've discussed the importance of putting a psychic shield of light around you before you begin the Akashic Record journeys in the Mindstream. These next exercises offer different ways to create a protective light around you which will help you feel stronger when dealing with challenging people or situations. Feeling safe in our bodies and in the world is essential and can be especially challenging for highly sensitive people. These next few exercises will help you to create shields around yourself and your energy field so you can move forward with greater strength and ease.

Mirrored Ball Exercise

A good add on to the beautiful place in nature journey you did earlier in this chapter is to include what I call the mirrored ball exercise. This is a fantastic visionary exercise you can do anytime you feel you're being subjected to negative vibrations or you want to ensure you're sending out only positive thoughts to others.

Exercise

Go back through the relaxation in the previous exercise and return to the space in nature.

Sitting against your personal tree, imagine noticing the golden ball of light is there, still surrounding you by about three feet in all directions. Know this light is still protecting you, healing you, and within it, only that which is of your highest good can come through.

Now that you notice the familiar golden light, we're going to add another layer. Imagine a stream of mirrored paint pouring down over that golden light ball, coating the light that is surrounding you. Allow that mirrored paint to completely cover the golden ball and create a mirrored shield around your body. Very good. Know that this mirror is sending your love out into the world and that whatever is being sent to you from others will be reflected back to the sender. If people send you love, they receive love. If people send less than positive thoughts toward you, those same thoughts will return and not affect you as you continue to intend to send light and love to all you encounter, now and always. Feel yourself surrounded by this mirrored shell and know that within this mirrored shell and golden light, you are completely protected from the energy of others. When you're ready, come back to waking consciousness carrying this shield with you.

***

Remember to use the mirrored ball anytime you feel your outer world is becoming overwhelming or if people or situations are pulling your core energy away from you.

Violet Light Shield Exercise

If you feel you need more than the mirror alone, violet light is incredibly transformational tool for psychic protection that is quite effective for shifting lower frequency vibrations. Return to your Waiting Room and the beautiful space in nature and surround yourself with the mirrored ball of protection. Once that's established, continue with the following.

Exercise

Now surrounding that mirrored shell, imagine a thick ball of violet light is surrounding you and the frequency of that light is getting higher and higher and higher, lighter and brighter. Allow that violet light to add another layer between you and the energies of others and know that today, all people you speak to will be pleasant and helpful and all energies will be for your highest good.

***

How did you feel in the violet light? I've found the violet shield is one of the fastest ways to shift unwanted influences. Like many of these exercises, they're easy to do anytime you need an energetic pick-me-up. You can also add the violet light to any journey taken into the Akashic Records to clear your energy field in preparation for other work.

Protective Shield and Hologram Exercise

Another creative way to shield and protect yourself from unwanted influences is by going through your doorway into the Mindstream, connecting with a hologram of yourself, and allowing that hologram to show up in certain places so people won't know exactly where you're at or what you're doing. Again, because the Akashic Records are nonlinear and presuppose that all time is now, this hologram confirms the idea that you can be in more than one place at any given time. To get there, take the following steps:

Exercise

Close your eyes and bring the Astral Light through your body from head to feet. Surround yourself with a golden bubble of light and imagine that light extends at least three to five feet around your body, making it far wider than normal. When you're ready, go through the door into your Waiting Room. Your guide is there with you and the two of you will now go together into your beautiful space in nature and all the way back to your favorite tree.

Standing with your back against the tree, feeling safe and secure, imagine you can invite a carbon copy of yourself to join you there. Know that this is a hologram of you. Notice you are still surrounded by golden light so you're completely safe and protected. Likewise, notice now that your holographic double is also protected and surrounded by a shield of pure white light.

Imagine you can allow this hologram of yourself to represent you energetically so that anyone who is sending you anything other than love and light will only see this hologram of you, rather than your real self. By having the attention of others focused on your hologram, you will be free to move around in life, free from the unwanted influences of others. Take a moment now to allow you and your guide to explain to the hologram what you'd like them to do on your behalf.

[**pause**]

When you're ready, thank your hologram and take your guide by the hand. Walk back through the beautiful space in nature and walk through the door and go back inside your Waiting Room. Be there now. Thank your guide for helping you today and turn and walk out the door where you first came in. You're back where you started, still surrounded by your protective golden light. Know that within this light that only that which is of your highest good can come through. In a moment when I count back from three, you will return, feeling awake and better than ever before. Three, grounded, centered and balanced; two, knowing that only your highest good can come through this shield of light you now have around you; and one, you're back!

***

How do you feel? Isn't it an interesting idea to set an intention that your double will shield you from the outer world? I've used this myself a few times, though not often. The big takeaway with any of these psychic shields is to do what is needed to establish a sense of strength within and to project it to the outer world.

GRIEF RECOVERY FOR A DECEASED LOVED ONE

Next up, we will make use of the vast storehouse of energy and information from the Akashic Records to help with one of the most important aspects of our current lives that is without a doubt one of the most painful parts of life—losing a loved one. The soul is limitless and timeless; in this exercise, you will access a room within the Akashic space where you can meet with a dearly departed loved one to finish conversations and gain insights and healing.

Working with many clients through the years taught me that one of the biggest obstacles to our grief recovery is the idea that our loved one is now separate from ourselves and that pain of being disconnected is tough to take. In this journey, you will reconnect with your loved one energetically to create a new state of peace. Meeting your beloved in the Mindstream is possible, again, because there is no such thing as time. The soul lives on, and you can easily meet with your loved one to have a meaningful and healing experience.

Exercise

Go through your process to connect with the Astral Light, surround yourself by your golden protective shield and enter your Waiting Room where you can greet your guide. Tell your guide that you're here today to experience a reunion with one of your loved ones who has crossed over into spirit. Take your time to explain your intention. Who are you planning to meet, or are you open to being surprised by who shows up? Take your time and tell your guide anything they need to know to assist you.

When you're ready, your guide shows you a doorway on the other side of your Waiting Room. Take your guide by the hand and go together to open the door. Find yourselves inside another high frequency room. A doorway is opening on the other side of that new room, and here comes your loved one. Notice now that they're walking or floating up to you. Know that this is their soul, their higher self. They appear totally healthy, happy, and so glad to see you, no matter how they were in physical life.

Take a moment now to imagine that you could put your arms around them and just hold them. Allow every cell of your body to totally reconnect with their energy now. Starting from the tips of your toes, cells are opening and expanding and relaxing, filling with light and the peace of knowing your loved one is with you again. You are remembering the feeling you had when they were here, and you know now that they are still right here, right now! They were never gone; the separation is an illusion. Allow yourself to realize that they are closer to you than you had thought. Feel the relief of no longer being separated from the love of this special person. Feel your entire body relax into this feeling as they hold you and you reconnect. Take your time.

[pause]

Once you feel totally reconnected to your loved one, imagine you can stand back and look at them. Go ahead and talk with them about anything you'd like to say and allow them to tell you what they need to say. If either of you wants to apologize, imagine you can both forgive each other. Discuss anything you need to and take your time.

[pause]

Very nice. Now thank them for joining you here today. Imagine they are so light and bright that they can now float away and return through the door they entered. You are so light and bright that you can take your guide by the hand and go back through the door into your Waiting Room. Thank your guide for helping you reconnect with your loved one and notice how much lighter you feel now.

When you're ready, leave your Waiting Room and go back to where you started. By the time I count back from three, you will return feeling awake, refreshed, and better than before. Three, grounded and balanced; two, feeling the light of reconnection now and always; and one, you're back!

✷✷✷

Did you meet the person you expected to see? Do you feel better now that you've energetically reconnected? What did they share with you that you can hold on to as you move into your future? Energetically resolving grief can truly help you in your present lifetime.

SOUL RETRIEVAL

Akashic Records give us information about our soul journey throughout time. Your soul is limitless and eternal, and yet, through trauma and challenge, our soul can become fragmented over time when we make various vows and agreements with our fellow beings. How can we heal from these past challenges? Our next process will help! Soul retrieval is one of the most powerful processes I know. The idea of the retrieval is to pick up pieces of ourselves that we've inadvertently scattered around during our current life journey through various relationships and hardships. Likewise, we may also carry things that are burdens we inadvertently chose to hang on to for others. Sometimes these things weigh us down and block us from fulfilling certain aspects of our soul's purpose. In this journey, you will meet with a loved one and give back what does not belong to you or what is no longer serving you, and take back or receive things that are for your highest good. This is all done in the theater of the mind, of course, but it can be truly self-empowering and can create incredible shifts in your outer world.

Exercise

Begin in your familiar place by closing your eyes and drawing upon the Astral Light and universal light of compassion. Bring the loving light through your entire body and allow yourself to connect with the heavens and the core of the earth. Surround yourself with golden light and enter the doorway to your Waiting Room.

Greet your guide and discuss your intention for this soul retrieval. Who are you planning to meet and why? Might you be surprised and allow someone who is for your highest good to show up? Your guide will assist you today in exchanging energy and information that will be most for your highest good at this moment in time. There's a doorway on the other side of the Waiting Room. Take your guide by the hand and walk toward the door. Open it and find yourself inside a sacred, peaceful room. Feel the supportive and loving energies of this space.

Inside this peaceful area, feeling safe and secure and accompanied by your guide, you notice that somebody who is very special to you is walking up to you now. The person may be alive now, or it may be someone who has already passed into spirit. Say hello and thank them for visiting you today. Imagine that this is the higher self or soul of the person talking to your higher self. Imagine you could take a moment now to thank each other for all of the lessons you came here to learn. If necessary, imagine you could apologize to each other for any misunderstandings and take time to discuss anything else that may need to be said.

Go ahead and ask them if they have anything that belongs to you, and if so, have them put whatever it is out on their hands so you can see it. Notice what's there. It may be a physical object or it could be a virtue such as love, or courage, or strength. Notice what they have for you now and if you have questions about what it is, ask them to clarify, or your guide can assist you.

Imagine now you know what they have for you. Ask them what this represents. Wait for their answer. How do you feel about what they're giving you? In a moment when I count to three, I want you to reach out and take what they've brought to you. Ready? One, two and three, imagine you can reach out now and bring that item back inside yourself. That's right. Go ahead and put it back inside. Very good! Now imagine your guide is sending a bright healing white light down through the top of your head. Allow the light to move into every single cell of your body, helping you heal and integrate this new energy you received today. The light is making you feel lighter and brighter than ever before.

Look within yourself and see if you have anything that belongs to them, that you've been carrying for them that is no longer serving you, or that is no longer for your highest good. Notice that now. What is it? What does it represent? When I count to three, your guide will help you release that and give it back to the person you're meeting with today. Ready? One, two and three, they're picking it up now. Notice now that they are taking this from you, and as they do, you are both getting lighter and brighter and you're both receiving this healing light. Very good!

Taking your time while this healing continues, discuss anything else that needs to be said. When you're ready, say goodbye, take your guide by the hand and walk back through the door and into your Waiting Room. Be back now, inside your special sacred space.

Thank your loving guide for assisting you again, and turn around and leave your Waiting Room and go back out to where you started. In a moment, when I count back from three, you'll return into the room feeling lighter and refreshed. Ready? Three, continuing to process this healing tonight so by tomorrow morning, you'll be fully integrated into this new energy, two, grounded, centered and balanced, and one, you're back!

***

How did you do? What did you receive, if anything? Did you receive physical objects or more spiritual gifts? What did you give back, if anything? Were you surprised by who showed up? Opening the door in the Mindstream to meet with other souls to finish up old business has the potential to positively affect the Akashic Records not only now, but in the future and past as well. When you heal something, past lives you may have shared with someone else are eased and any future lifetimes will be healthier and more complete as a result of your efforts. I've found soul retrievals to be one of the most incredible things you can do for yourself to revitalize your life force and move forward in a positive new direction.

TAKING YOUR HEART BACK

Another version of the soul retrieval is taking back your heart. You may have already received your heart during that last exercise, or you may not even realize you've given your heart away either to an ex-partner or another person such as a parent or caregiver. Years ago when I ventured into the Akashic Records and did a similar exercise, I discovered that I gave my heart to someone who passed away years earlier. The moment I retrieved my heart, I felt better physically. It's unbelievable how beneficial this can be for your physical vitality, even though this is obviously taking place in the realm of what we would deem our imagination. Astral Light—also called Aether or Akasha—is a very real space even though it is nonphysical. Changing things there matters.

Taking your heart back can make incredible improvements in your life. Then again, once you go there, you may discover that you don't need to do this, as you may not have actually given your heart away at all. Finding out is still beneficial.

What I've found is that many people have given their hearts to others, and yet this is outside their conscious awareness. They could have done so out of love, or perhaps they share a soul contract with the recipient. Choosing to go and ask for your heart back is incredibly self-empowering. If this is something you need, you'll be glad you did. As I mentioned during the last exercise, when someone is holding your heart, you have karma between the two of you that will live on in the Akashic Records, whether you're aware of it or not. To move forward in future lives in a clear way while energetically clearing up past karma from either this life or former incarnations, taking the heart back can prove invaluable. When setting your intentions for this journey, you may want to ask your higher self if you need this journey. If so, see who shows up for you without setting specific expectations about who that might be. Sometimes people get big surprises that are completely out of their conscious awareness. You may consciously assume one person has your heart, for example, but the journey reveals someone you hadn't even thought about. That's why in this case, it's best to keep the journey a bit flexible and see what happens. Ready? Let's go find out.

Exercise

Go into your relaxed state by drawing the Astral Light through your body and surrounding yourself with a golden protective ball of light. Go through the door and into your Waiting Room where you can meet your guide. Explain to your guide that you intend to find out if there's anyone out there who has your heart. If so, you've come here today to take your heart back in accordance with your highest good. Notice the same door you went through before to retrieve things that belong to you. Know that even if you are still in possession of your heart, you will take the journey to meet with someone who has something of value to return to you today. Go with your guide, safe and protected, inside that room again.

This time, you find another person has appeared there. Again, you recognize that this is the higher self or soul of someone who has played an important role in your soul journey. Imagine they've joined you today to give back something important that belongs to you. Notice what they're returning to you. Notice the first thought that appears in your mind as you either look at your heart or feel that it's there. If it is not your heart, notice what the person has chosen. Allow them to explain the significance of this item and speak with them about why they're giving it back to you.

If they are offering you your heart, when you're ready and with your guide's help, when I count to three in a moment, you will pick up your heart and place it in your body, right where your heart should go. Ready? One, two, and three, you're picking up your heart and bringing it back inside, noticing your heart is now back where it belongs. Very good.

If the person has brought something else, notice and allow yourself to energetically reconnect with that object or energy now if it is for your highest good.

Regardless of what you received, as you connect with the item, imagine your guide is sending you a healing light that comes down through the top of your head and moves down into your heart center. Imagine the light is like a welder's torch that reconnects your spiritual heart with your physical heart. This light is mending any cracks or breaks in your heart and molding your heart into a state of total perfection. Your heart is now filled with light and that light is getting brighter and brighter and brighter, lighter and lighter. Take your time. Very good.

Notice how much better you feel now that you have your heart or other item back. Notice how complete you feel. Allow that healing light to continue to work for however long you need. As you do that, I want you to notice if you have anything that belongs to them. If you do, offer it in your hands. It may be their heart or something else, or perhaps you don't have anything that belongs to them. If nothing specific appears, go ahead and give them love and light.

On the count of three, they will take whatever they need to receive from you today. Ready? One, two, and three, they're taking whatever you've given them and are bringing that energy inside their own heart. Notice how much lighter you feel now that you've given that energy to them. The weight of the world is gone. Allow the healing white light to move through the other person and give them the same type of healing you received a moment ago. Now imagine the light moving once again through you and filling in the space previously occupied by whatever you gave back. Notice how much better you feel. Very good!

Take a moment to ask this person any additional questions you need to gain further clarity. When you're ready, take your guide by the hand and return through the door and go back into your Waiting Room. Thank your guide for assisting you today and go out the door where you entered, closing that door behind you. Be back in the space where you started. When I count back from three, you will return to full waking consciousness. Three, allowing this healing to continue for as long as needed and knowing now that you are grounded, centered, and balanced; two, still surrounded by golden, healing light, knowing that within this light, only that which is of highest good can come through; and one, you're back!

***

Who showed up for you that time? Did you discover your heart or were you given something else? Did you give the other person anything besides love and light? Can you see how such an exchange would have a positive impact on your soul within the Akashic Records? How might this exchange clear up any old karma for you in the future? How can you experience more peace and energy in your current lifetime as a result of this exchange? Each step you take in self-understanding and awareness is bound to create more room for joy in your life journey.

COSMIC TRASH CAN

I want to share one of my favorite exercises with you. Years ago, while wandering in the Mindstream to peek at the Akashic Records, I discovered a powerful tool in the Cosmic Trash Can. I often have clients imagine a giant trash can where they can unload all their emotional baggage and difficulties. With the help of your spirit guide, you will not believe how much lighter you will feel after going through this short process. Again, by taking the trash out once in a while, your Akashic Records become clearer in past, present, and future. Ready to try this?

Exercise

Close your eyes and allow the Astral Light to travel from head to toe. Surround yourself with golden light and walk into your Waiting Room. Your guide is there waiting for you and has shown up today with a giant trashcan or dumpster that has unlimited capacity. In a moment, you can begin reaching inside yourself and pulling out anything that is no longer serving you or energy that does not belong to you. If you need help deciding what to let go of, take a moment and speak with your guide or simply allow yourself to release whatever is needed in accordance with your highest good.

[**pause**]

Now imagine you can reach inside yourself and pull out this old energy. Put it into the trash. Take your time. Dig into yourself. Even if you don't know exactly what it is you're throwing out, just know that you can lighten up and rid yourself of whatever your higher self and your guide feel is no longer serving you. As you continue to place this old material in the trash, feel how much lighter you're becoming as a result of your work. Take your time.

[**pause**]

When you're finished, imagine your guide is closing the lid on the can or dumpster. Imagine also an energetic cord of light coming out of your stomach or solar plexus area that is connecting you with all the stuff you just threw away. Your guide is now pulling out a big pair of golden scissors. In a moment when I count to three, your guide will cut that cord and release you completely from that old garbage. Ready? One, two, and three, your guide is cutting that cord, lifting that trash, no matter how big it is, up into the air and tossing it out into outer space where it disintegrates into a bazillion tiny pieces. Imagine that a loving, healing light is pouring down from above and moving in through that cut cord. The loving light is filling in the space previously occupied by that old energy. You're now getting lighter and lighter and lighter, brighter and brighter. Very nice!

When you're ready, thank your guide for helping you with this today. Know you can return anytime you need to take out the trash. Go back to the door and out to where you began. When I count back from three, you will return feeling lighter and better than ever before. Three, awake and refreshed; two, being safe in all activities; and one, you're back!

***

How much lighter do you feel now? Isn't it incredible? Can you see how lightening your soul's burdens in this way will help you have clearer Akashic Records in the future? I've used the Cosmic Trash Can so many times through the years for clients and myself; I know firsthand that this can be a huge help At times, you won't even realize how much stuff you're carrying around until it's gone. You may find yourself feeling lighter and better than ever, which is my hope for you.

SUMMING UP

Life is what you make it. Often perception creates reality, so by having the courage to dig deep and identify places in need of healing, you can create the positive life you truly want and deserve. Once you address the challenges in current life situations, accessing other areas in the Mindstream becomes much easier. Fantastic job!

Chapter Eight

DISCOVERING YOUR SOUL'S PURPOSE WITHIN THE AKASHIC RECORDS

One of the main reasons a person seeks a past-life regression or any other kind of spiritual healing session is to discover their unique soul's purpose. Because your soul's purpose is something you've been doing over many, many lifetimes, discovering your purpose is one of the best uses and reasons for accessing the Akashic Records. Each person is here on this earth at this very time for a reason. Seekers yearn to experience firsthand what that entails and the knowledge and self-understanding you'll receive in these next exercises are designed to do just that. Enjoy!

JOURNEY TO FIND YOUR SOUL'S PURPOSE

One of the best reasons to do journey work is to confront the reason you're here. In past-life regression sessions, lessons or dominating patterns tend to stay with the soul over the course of their existence, and discovering that information can prove quite profound. In this next exercise, your guide will help you uncover your main soul's purpose.

Exercise

Sit or lie down in a comfortable place where you won't be disturbed. Connect your energy with the Astral Light and allow that beam of pure white light to permeate every single cell in your body. Allow an illuminating golden glow to surround you and know that you are protected within that golden shell. Walk or float through the door and go into your Waiting Room. See your guide there and let them know that today, you need assistance in uncovering your dominant soul's purpose. You may have many lessons you're learning in life, but you now ask about the most important theme or purpose your soul wants to experience and has been experiencing over the course of many, many lifetimes. Explain any additional thoughts and take a moment to conclude this request.

[**pause**]

When you're ready, your guide asks you to accompany them to the other side of the room where there's another door. That door is opening now, and you and your guide are going inside a beautiful room. Notice what's there. Is this furnished with homey items, or is this more of an office, for example? However it looks, you feel very safe and relaxed here. Your guide is escorting you to a place where you can sit comfortably. Go ahead and sit with them. If your guide needs to show you anything that relates to your soul purpose, imagine they can bring that out now or they can simply sit and tell you all the details of your dominant soul's purpose. So what is your soul's purpose? Notice the first thought that comes into your mind. How long has this purpose been in play in your soul's history? If you've had this purpose in other lifetimes, imagine your guide can tell you about those other lifetimes. What event or events triggered this dominant purpose? How are you fulfilling your purpose in your current lifetime? What improvements or changes could you make to better fulfill your purpose? Take your time, and know your guide is happy to answer any and all questions.

[pause]

When you're finished, rise from your seat and follow your guide back through this room to the door and go back into your Waiting Room. Thank your guide for helping you today. Say goodbye for now and go back out the door you first entered. In a moment, when I count back from three, you will return. Three, grounded, centered, and balanced; two, fully understanding your reason for being and allowing any other insights to come to you overnight so by tomorrow morning, you will be clear; and one, you're back!

***

Were you surprised by your purpose? My past clients were often shocked at the sheer simplicity of their purpose. Life is not always as complex as we try to make it. Many people report that their purpose is to love, to learn to forgive, or to be happy, for example. Through the Akashic Records, those same themes run through many past lives and may continue on into the future. Whatever your purpose, I wish you joy as you continue to manifest your purpose in your lifetime.

MEETING YOUR SOULMATES

The concept of soulmates is often confusing and misunderstood. Hopeless romantics purport your soulmate is a single person you're meant to meet and, once that happens, the two of you will live happily ever after like a happy couple in a Hallmark Channel movie. That sounds amazing, but in reality, life doesn't always run so smoothly. Also, we may encounter more than one person who could be a suitable life partner.

Likewise, soulmates come in many forms. We may have several different kinds of soulmates who come into our lives. Some soulmates are kind and helpful friends, while others may actually show up as foes, or people who throw a wrench into our plans. Such soulmates step in to help us *not* get what we *thought* we wanted. When things go awry, we typically label the experience as negative, yet sometimes in hindsight find ourselves feeling so very thankful when our wishes *don't* come true. Haven't you found that to be the case? I think everyone goes through that at least a few times in life. Contrary to popular belief, often our most challenging relationships involve souls who love us the most on a *soul level*. Such people are in our lives to push our buttons on purpose so we succeed in learning life's biggest lessons.

Regardless of what kind of soulmate you hope to encounter, this next journey will help you come face to face with the important people in your life so you can share meaningful conversations with their higher selves and find resolution to tough challenges between you.

Exercise

Sit in your familiar and comfortable space. Breathe in through your nose, exhale out your mouth. Relax and close your eyes. Feel the loving embrace of the Astral Light as it moves through the top of your head and into every single cell in your being. Feel that light wash away any tensions you have as it moves toward your feet, connecting you with earth and sky. Feel the light rush out of your heart center, creating your beautiful bright golden ball of protective light that will surround you by several feet in all directions. When you're ready, walk through the door to your Waiting Room and meet your guide. Say hello and let your guide know that you'd like to have a meaningful conversation with any and all soulmates you've chosen in your current lifetime. Ask your guide to bring your awareness to any people you most need to meet. Take your time to explain any other nuances you'd like to explore during your time together. You may think of specific people or simply request that whomever needs to show up for your highest good can be present.

[pause]

When you're both ready, take your guide's hand and move across your Waiting Room to a doorway on the other side of the room. Open the door and go with your guide to another lovely living room or sitting area. Feel the peaceful energy here as you explore before taking a seat. Notice a doorway on the other side of the room. That door is opening now, and here come some of your soulmates who are here to assist you with your life lessons in your current lifetime. Who's there? Notice everything about them, say hello, and as you do, imagine they are all happy to see you, even if that's not how they behave in waking life. Know that what you see now are their higher selves or souls; regardless of what kind of relationship you have in your current life, they are happy to see you, they feel loving toward you, and you sense the unconditional love and high regard they have for you as a soul in this interdimensional and neutral space.

One by one, I want you to speak to each person and ask them some questions. What purpose do they play in your life? What lessons are they helping you learn? You may have a wonderful relationship. If so, discuss that now and why it is so important to you both. If either of you need to apologize for any wrongdoing, do so now. They may let you know that the things they did were part of your learning, yet they are still sorry. If at all possible, forgive them. If you need to apologize to them, do that now. Notice if they could also forgive you. Discuss any ways in which the two of you could move forward in a more productive and supportive way. If the person truly loves you in your daily life, let them also share what purpose they have for being in your life. Allow them to tell you how much they appreciate you, and do the same if you feel so guided. Take your time, say whatever needs to be said. If your guide needs to step in for any clarification, allow them to do so. Meanwhile, move through these meaningful conversations with each person who joined you today.

[pause]

Once you're finished, imagine each of them can say goodbye and watch while they walk or float back through the door where they came in. Take a moment to discuss what happened with your guide.

[pause]

When you're ready, follow your guide back through the room and open the door, returning to your Waiting Room. Thank your guide for assisting you today. When you're ready, say goodbye and go back through the doorway you entered, and out to where you started. In a moment, when I count down from three, you will return, feeling better than ever before. Three, grounded, centered, and balanced; two, processing all of the learning in your sleep so that by tomorrow you will feel lighter than ever before; and one, you're back!

Who showed up for you and identified themselves as your soulmates? Were you surprised by who met you there? Were the people pleasant, or did some of your challenging relationships show up also? What can you learn from this meeting to improve your relationships moving forward? Who would you like to see next time you do this exercise?

SOUL CONTRACTS

No doubt there are people around us whom we've been with before; the previous exercise on soulmates certainly suggests that is the case. We often enter into soul contracts, prearranged before our arrival in our current lifetime, where we make plans to meet certain people at certain predestined moments. Beyond the general learning our soulmates provide, sometimes we agree to play out certain things for people to help them grow, or they assist our spiritual growth through life lessons. I'd love to say these lessons are all fun and games, but as you probably know, that's simply not the case. The soul contracts we make can be incredibly challenging to handle. We come into our earthly life to help others and to learn and evolve our souls. Unfortunately, many of us need tough lessons in order to achieve change. When we consciously work on ourselves through meditation or by undergoing past life regression, we gain understanding of who we are, why we're here, and what we decided to learn before our arrival. We can also come to an understanding of which souls are with us who we've perhaps been with in other lifetimes to discover the specific contracts we have with these folks. Knowing what your contracts are and whether or not they can be paid in full can provide you with empowering experiences for helping you take back your personal power and moving forward. The sole reason for doing self-reflective work is to hopefully clear up some of these loose ends and resolve issues so you can move forward in your current life experience with greater peace such that if you do incarnate again in the future, you will have a more peaceful experience. This next exercise will help you learn more about such agreements.

Exercise

Sit in a comfortable place and allow the Astral Light to move through your body. See a golden ball of healing light that surrounds you by about three feet in all directions. Walk through the door into your Waiting Room. See your guide there and let them know that today, you would like to know if you made any soul contracts either earlier in your current lifetime or in past lives, and if so, you'd like to know exactly what they are and if any of them need to be revoked. Know your guide will assist you in discovering any soul contracts that would be for your highest good. Take a moment to speak to your guide about this matter and discuss any other intentions.

[**pause**]

When ready, follow your guide to the other side of the room where you see another door. That door is opening now, and you and your guide are entering a beautiful room. This may be the same room you went to earlier when you discovered your soul's purpose, or it may be new; either way, notice what's there. Feel the peaceful energy of the space and know you're safe and relaxed here. Your guide asks you to take a seat. As you sit, your guide is walking to another part of this room and returns a moment later. Notice whether your guide is holding any files. Maybe, maybe not. Know that these files represent current soul contracts. If not, take a moment to discuss why you don't have any soul contracts.

If your guide has any files to share with you, allow your guide to go through each one and explain them to you. Take your time. What contracts do you have? How long have you had them? When did you make them and why? Which agreements are no longer serving you? If they're not needed or not serving you, would it be okay to shred them or rip them up now and call them complete? If so, allow your guide to help you bring these matters to completion by shredding any unnecessary contracts and helping you dispose of them. Take all the time you need to do this process.

[pause]

When you're finished, return any remaining files to your guide and wait while they put them away. When they return, rise from your seat and follow your guide back through the room to the door. Open the door and return to your Waiting Room. Thank your guide for helping you today. Say goodbye for now and leave through the door you first entered. In a moment, when I count back from three, you will return. Three, grounded, centered, and balanced; two, fully understanding your reason for being and allowing any other insights to come to you overnight so that by tomorrow morning, you will be clear; and one, you're back!

Did you have contracts? Were there any you could complete or do you still have some in play? There's no right or wrong if some are still active when you finish the journey. Some of our experiences are meant to stretch out for a lifetime while other situations are only temporary.

SPIRITUAL VOWS

Spiritual vows aren't the same kind of promise you make on your wedding day. These are widespread proclamations that your soul made in a past life that can either bless you or wreak havoc on what you're trying to create in your current life. Vows are often uncovered by accident during a typical past-life regression. You can also take command by proactively traveling to the space in the Mindstream where you can access the records of your vows, if you have any. In this next exercise, you'll be able to find out whether or not you made vows or other binding agreements in the distant past. As with many of these exercises, it might be best to inquire about what is for your highest good because you might be surprised by what shows up. Likewise, you may discover that you don't have any vows at all; that knowledge is just as powerful.

Exercise

Close your eyes and connect your energy with the Astral Light and your protective golden shell of light. Walk through the door to your Waiting Room. See your guide there and let them know that today you need assistance to determine if you have any vows you made, particularly if those vows are causing difficulty in your current lifetime.

[pause]

When you're ready, follow your guide to the door on the other side of the room. That door is opening now, and you and your guide are entering a beautiful room. Again, this may be a familiar place or it may be new. Either way, know that here you are safe, secure, and you feel incredibly relaxed. Go through the room with your guide and take a seat. If your guide needs to show you anything that relates to any vows your soul made, imagine they can bring that out now. They may have documents or other items relating to vows. Notice whatever you notice, or you may find you don't have any vows at this moment. Allow your guide to explain all the details of any vows you made in the past. Feel free to ask about the information you received. Do you have any vows? If so, what are they? What year did you make these vows, notice the first thought that comes into your mind. What purpose did the vow serve? Can you resolve these issues now, or should the vow remain intact? Discuss this with your guide as to whether any vows need to be deemed null and void; if so, ask how you can go about doing so. If some vows are about things you want, discover that and know you can be at peace about your decision.

[pause]

When you're finished, allow your guide to put back any items you found in their places. The two of you will now walk together through the room to the door and go back into your Waiting Room. Thank your guide for helping you today. Say goodbye and leave through the door you first entered. In a moment when I count back from three, you will return. Three, grounded, centered, and balanced; two, releasing any residual energies from unwanted vows overnight so by tomorrow morning you will be clear; and one, you're back!

Did you discover any vows? If so, how were they affecting your current life? Do you feel you gained insight and resolution from the journey? Great job!

BEFORE YOU ARRIVED

One of my favorite in-between areas of the Mindstream is a high frequency dimension that exists shortly before we incarnate in our current lifetime. In that space, we each made some agreements, or let's say we picked up your rental car and hotel reservations and received a vague roadmap for the journey we were about to embark upon in this current lifetime. This information can be incredibly helpful and insightful. Let's go on the journey and find out exactly what you planned before you arrived.

Exercise

Return to your safe and comfortable space where you do your journey work. Sit down and close your eyes. Breathe in healing and peace and light, and exhale any tensions. Connect with the Astral Light and allow that light to move through your body, beginning with the top of your head, your face and neck, your shoulders, your arms and hands, and imagine the light moves down your spine toward your heart center. Keep breathing in this loving energy as the light continues to move through your body to the base of your spine and down into your legs, knees, ankles, and the soles of your feet. Extend that light through the feet and imagine it travels to the center of the earth. Feel your body existing between earth and sky and know that all is well.

When you're ready, notice how the light intensifies, surrounding you with a golden ball of light. Know that as always, within this golden light, you are safe, secure and protected. Notice the doorway you've been through before that leads into your Waiting Room. Open the door, walk into the room, and notice your guide. Let your guide know that today you'd like to learn exactly what your soul planned before you arrived in your current lifetime. Take your time to discuss any other issues with your loving friend.

[**pause**]

When you're ready, you and your guide will walk or float to the other side of your Waiting Room where you will find an inviting elevator. Notice the elevator and push the Up button. The doors open, and you and your guide step into the elevator. As you do, notice the control panel and the button at the very top. That button will take you far out of the third dimension and into a space between your earthly lives. Push that button now and you and your guide will go up, up, up, higher and higher, up into this new dimension in time and space. In a moment when I count to three, your elevator will stop. One, ascending higher than ever before; two, further and further, noticing that the higher up you go, the more relaxed and peaceful you feel; and one, you're there. Your elevator stops and the doors open. You and your guide step out and find yourselves in a space filled with the highest frequency pure white light that you have ever encountered. Feel the incredible energy as you and your guide float in this expansive light.

Move through the area and imagine that up ahead, there's a being of pure white light there to greet you. Go ahead and say hello. Feel the unconditional love this being has for you.

Let the being know your request today, which is: "I would like to meet with my creator to discuss the plans I made right before I arrived in my current lifetime."

The being acknowledges this request and asks you to follow them through this space. Notice ahead is another elevator. Go up to the elevator and watch as the being pushes the Up button and the doors open. The being is welcoming you and your guide into the elevator. Once again, notice the control panel and push the highest button you can. The elevator doors close and you find yourself moving up, up, up. By the time I count to three, you will arrive to this area far beyond time and space. Ready? One, two, three, you're there. Be there now and allow the doors to open. You and your guide will step out and into another room with even higher frequencies than the one you were in before.

Follow your guide into this incredible space, and as you do, a doorway on the other side of the room is opening now and a stunningly beautiful being of pure white light is moving toward you. This being is the creator, the All That Is, who knows everything about you, your soul, and all beings and creations in all universes. There is nothing they don't know. Feel the unconditional love this being feels toward you. Allow the loving light of their presence to wash away any heavy energy you may have had before today. Go ahead now and tell this loving presence why you're here—to receive details about the plan you made for your current lifetime. Ask the being any questions about the plan. What did you most want to learn at a soul level? What experiences did you choose and why? Allow the being to explain everything to you now. Take your time to receive all the information you need.

[**pause**]

Can you see how your life up to this point is a perfect reflection of what you chose to experience? What influences will you keep with you moving forward? What can you release in order to move forward with greater ease? What plans did you make that perhaps have not yet manifested? How can you bring those to fruition in a way that will bring the greatest happiness to you and all concerned? Continue discussing this with the All That Is for as long as you need and know that your personal guide can also assist you in understanding the complexities of your soul's journey.

[**pause**]

When you're ready, thank this loving presence for helping you today. Continue to feel the total and complete unconditional love emanating from them. Go with your guide and return to the elevator. The doors open and you and your personal guide will press the lowest button you can which will take you all the way back to your Waiting Room. Ready? Going down, down, down, leaving these higher dimensions as you return to earth, noticing you are filled with the peace of knowledge and understanding. Grounding yourself through the light cord in the soles of your feet, you feel yourself moving back toward the earth. By the time I count to three, you will be back in the third dimension. One, moving down through time and space; two, grounding yourself to earth; and three, you're back.

The elevator doors open and you and your guide are now back inside your Waiting Room. Be there now and exit the elevator. Take a moment to get any other perspectives from your guide and ask your guide for clarification on today's journey.

[pause]

When you're ready, thank your guide for assisting you and turn and walk out the door. Be back where you started, surrounded by golden healing light. Find yourself filled with the high frequency energy from these other dimensions, filled with greater peace, knowing the path that your soul has chosen. You understand your life is unfolding exactly how you planned. In a moment when I count back from five, you will return to the present moment feeling awake, refreshed, and better than ever before. Five, you're grounded, centered and balanced; four, continuing to process this information in your dreams tonight so by tomorrow morning you will be fully integrated into this new level of self-understanding; three, driving safely and being safe in all activities; two, grounded, centered, and balanced; and one, you're back!

How did you enjoy your trip to meet with the creator of the universe? Did you feel the healing energy from that high frequency light? What did you learn about the plans you made? Were you surprised by what you discovered? Did you receive what you hoped? How have your current life events up to this point been a reflection of what you picked out before you arrived? Wonderful work! I hope you'll take some notes to keep track of your journey throughout your life and emerge knowing that your plans are unfolding exactly how they should in alignment with divine order.

CONNECTING WITH HEART'S DESIRE

What do we want in life? That's often a tough question. Next, we will do a continuation of the mystical journey through the forest from chapter five. This time, you will be assisted in connecting with your true heart's desire. Not sure what you truly want in your life? No problem. You'll find out here, and you may be surprised by what comes up! For that reason, I suggest asking for what's for highest good rather than specifics. Clients over the years have expressed great confusion about their real values and what they really want. You don't need to apologize for the desires of the heart. In this place, your soul can be free to express those ideas freely.

Exercise

Close your eyes and relax and bring the flow of Astral Light through your body as you connect with a green bubble of light. Walk into your Waiting Room, meet your guide, open the door on the other side of the room, and ascend the crystal staircase visited earlier in the section on spirit guides. Go now up the eight crystal stairs. Ready? One, two, three, four, five, so relaxed, six, seven, and eight, you're there. Find yourself back in that magical forest and connect with the creatures, beings and spirit guides who assist you with abundance.

Greet and follow these special guides down the path into the forest until you pass through the trees and into a clearing. In the distance is a table. Know that your heart's desire is on that table. You can't see it clearly yet, so allow your guides to take you there. Begin walking out into the middle of the clearing. Be there now. Look down at the table and notice what you see. Know that this is your heart's desire. Your heart's desire is right there in front of you.

Whatever you want most in the world is there and it's all yours. Reach your arms out, pick up your heart's desire and place it right inside your heart. Take a deep breath as you connect with your true heart's desire. Continue to stand around the table speaking with your guides. Allow them to tell you anything you need to know at this moment.

[**pause**]

Thank each of your guides for meeting you in this special place today, and watch them slowly walk away from you. Know that you're going to take your heart's desire with you and keep it with you always. Turn and walk through the clearing and go back into the forest, walking through the trees, notice some fairies, other creatures, a leprechaun, a sprite, or any nature spirits or animals. Walk or float back through the forest and find the crystal staircase once again. Go with your main guide and walk down the eight steps. Eight, seven six, five, four, three, two, and one, you're back and moving through the door to your Waiting Room. Be there now and ask your guide any other questions about your heart's desire.

[**pause**]

Thank your guide and walk through the door and return to where you started. You're still surrounded by green healing light, abundant and connected with your heart's desire. In a moment, when I count back from three, you will return. Three, grounded, centered, and balanced; two, processing this journey in your dreams so by tomorrow morning you will be prepared to be fully connected with your true desires; and one, you're back!

Were you surprised by your heart's desire? What steps can you take to connect with that feeling in your daily life? You may want to jot down notes about the specifics of the information you received. Great job!

SUMMING UP

Discovering your true, authentic self is a lifetime endeavor. Taking journeys to uncover the real purpose for your life can be incredibly uplifting and revealing. Understanding that all people who are in our lives are there for a reason, even when situations are challenging, can empower you to heal past hurts and powerfully persist on the road of life. Likewise, embracing those who truly love you is a great reminder that you're never alone on this life path.

We all made certain plans before we arrived. Although it's sometimes hard to see how things unfold, I hope these exercises have left you with the idea that you showed up here at this moment in time and space for a reason.

Chapter Nine

PAST LIVES IN THE MINDSTREAM

Ever since my early childhood, I have always believed that we lived before and that we will go on from here into a glorious afterlife, only to be reborn again at a time that is prearranged by our own soul, guides, and creator. One of the main pieces of information that exists within the Akashic Records are the documents and information relating to all of our past lives and the past lives of all beings who have ever existed. I'm sure everybody realizes how much I love to do guided imagery into past lives. I have several books on reincarnation that give you tons of past-life regression journeys, so in this section, I want to share some different past-life regression journeys to help you recall who you've been in the past. Enjoy!

RIVER IN TIME

Since the Mindstream implies a body of water, in this first journey, we're going to have you go to a space where you can float down a river of time to access details about your soul's journey.

Exercise

Sit in your comfortable space. Relax and close your eyes. Breathe in love and peace and healing, and exhale any tensions. Allow yourself to connect with the loving Astral Light. Bring the light down through the crown of your head as the light slowly moves into every single cell in your being, healing you and carrying away any stress. The light is moving through your arms, your torso, and your legs, and going out the soles of your feet. Imagine you can follow this light as it dives into the earth, grounding you. The light becomes so strong now, it connects you with earth and sky and begins to surround your body to form a golden ball of light. You're inside that protective bubble of golden light now where you are safe and secure always.

Notice your familiar doorway to your Waiting Room. Walk or float through that door now. Take a look around and notice how relaxed you feel here in your familiar place. Your guide is waiting for you. Say hello and tell your guide what your intention is for this journey down the river in time. What past-life details would you like to discover? Take a moment to discuss anything you need to with your guide.

[**pause**]

When you're ready, take your guide's hand and the two of you will begin to float toward a doorway on the other side of the room. Your guide opens that door now and you find yourselves in a bright white space. Up ahead is a rushing flow of light and a boat. Walk or float up to the boat. Notice what kind of boat it is—a canoe? A speedboat? A small ship? Notice whatever pops into your mind. When you're ready, you and your guide will climb aboard this boat and sail down this river. Ready? Go ahead and climb inside the boat. Know that this boat is on the river of time at a moment that represents the present day. In a moment, the boat will begin floating down the river. Know that the further down the river you float, the earlier the time will be. Allow yourselves to sail away now.

Floating back in time, you will now float over your earlier years, your childhood, past your birth in your current lifetime. Imagine the boat speeds up and begins floating even faster now as you and your guide float all the way back to the earliest time you can, to the most important event that your soul needs to experience that relates to the intention you set for your journey today.

You're floating so fast now, in a moment, when I count to three, you will arrive at this very early event. One, floating further back in time; two, further and further, going way, way, way back; and three, you're there. Be there now.

Your boat stops. Go with your guide and step off the boat. The moment you step ashore, imagine you can be in your previous life. Be there now and notice what year it is, the first thing that pops into your mind. Imagine now that the bright white light fades away and the details of your surroundings come fully into mind. Where are you? Notice the first thing that comes to your mind. How do you feel and what's happening? Imagine as you walk down the banks of this river of time, noticing these early events, you can move through the most significant events of your life in those early days. What lessons did you learn there? Why is this event important to the intention you set at the beginning of this journey? Take your time to notice whatever is for your highest good.

[pause]

When you're ready, take your guide by the hand, turn, and walk toward the river. Notice that the closer to the river you go, the bright white light reappears and the old surroundings you just visited fade away. Notice your boat ahead and climb aboard. The two of you will now begin to float forward in time, toward today. Moving swiftly with the current, you pass through the centuries and arrive where you began. Be there now. Exit the boat and move through the bright white light toward the door you came through. Open that door now and go inside your Waiting Room. Take your time to talk to your guide and discuss anything about this journey.

[pause]

When you're ready, thank your guide and move back to the door you first entered and step out to the place where your journey began. Be there now. When I count down from five, you will return feeling awake, refreshed, and better than ever before. Five, you're grounded, centered and balanced; four, processing all of this information in your dreams tonight so by tomorrow morning you will be fully integrated into this new information; three, driving and being safe in all of your activities; two, you're grounded and centered; and one, you're back!

***

How did you enjoy floating down the river of time? What lifetime did you experience? Did you receive new information you weren't expecting?

CLOSET WITH CLOTHES

One of my favorite ways to help clients access past life memories is by guiding them into a closet where they can see what they're wearing. The memories of clothing you wore in the past is most definitely stored within the Akashic Records, and you can experience it firsthand. When you can have a feeling of the clothes you wore in addition to visual cues, the depth of the experience can be truly profound. In this exercise, you can experience this for yourself.

Exercise

Sit in your familiar space and close your eyes. Bring the Astral Light down from the universe, through your body, arms, legs, and through your feet. Breathe and allow the light to surround you and form a golden ball of protective light.

You notice now your doorway is there. Walk through the door and into your Waiting Room. Your guide is there to greet you. Say hello and explain what you'd like to work on today: ask your guide to take you to see clothes you've worn in prior lifetimes.

[pause]

When you're ready, take your guide by the hand and cross the room together. Notice a door there. Your guide opens the door. As you look inside, you see a huge room. The room may contain all kinds of things. Notice what you notice and as you're taking a look around, you see a long rack of clothing that begins quite close to you and extends far into the distance. Your guide informs you now that these are all the clothes you have ever worn before, so this rack of clothes feels very safe, secure, and familiar to you. Now, walk past all of the items you have in your current closet. As you do, you notice that the clothing is getting older. You begin to notice items you used to own, then into things you had as a child, a baby, and that rack of clothes continues on and on. Know now that the further you walk, the older the clothes will be.

Ask your guide to help you find the appropriate clothes that relate to whatever you're asking about today. Taking your guide's hand, continue floating on and on, further and further, and when I count to three, you will arrive at the appropriate clothing. One, walking past the clothes; two, noticing what's there but continuing to follow your guide; and three, you've arrived. Some clothing lights up. Your guide hands them to you. Try them on now.

What are you wearing? What time period do these clothes come from? How do you feel in them? How old are you in those clothes? Notice these things and imagine you can take a few steps forward and find a door there. Open that door and step into that life wearing those clothes. Be there now. Notice what's happening. Allow yourself to move through the important events of your life when you wore those clothes to understand why this event relates to what you would like to learn about yourself.

[pause]

When you're sure you've received what you came for, turn and find your guide waiting for you. Walk or float to the door and find yourself back inside the room with the clothing rack. Your guide takes the clothes and hangs them up again. The two of you walk or float past all those clothes, back to the items you wore as a baby, as a child, and all the way to your current wardrobe. See the door you walked through. Open that door and find yourself in your Waiting Room. Thank your guide and ask for any clarification.

[pause]

When you're ready, leave your Waiting Room and go out to where you began. Still surrounded by golden healing light, when I count back from five in a moment, you will return feeling awake, refreshed, and better than before. Five, you're grounded, centered, and balanced; four, processing all of this in your dreams tonight; three, being safe in every activity; two; one; and you're back!

***

What clothes did you find? Why were they meaningful to the information you wanted to receive today? Definitely take some notes because you'll find them tremendously helpful down the road.

SCREEN JOURNEY

One of my new favorite ways to access past lives these days through what I call the Screen Journey. This screen can be any kind—a television, a phone, a tablet, a desktop—there are so many to choose from. Rather than becoming completely energetically immersed in the experience of being in your prior lifetimes, this process allows you to watch your former self in a video on a screen and receive pertinent information and subsequent healing as needed. The Screen Journey provides an incredibly safe space that's a little more removed yet still incredibly helpful to people recovering from big life challenges. Like all the other journeys in the book, the cosmic screen can be accessed from your Waiting Room. Remember to decide what you'd like to work on before you go. Ready to try this? Great!

Exercise

Go to your comfortable space, settle in, and close your eyes. Draw the peaceful Astral Light from the universe down through the top of your head, through your arms and hands, your torso, through your legs, and into your feet as that light moves down into the earth. Connect with earth and sky. Breathe. Notice your doorway in front of you. Open your Waiting Room door and step inside. Greet your guide.

Today your guide is going to assist you with uncovering some of your most important past lives. Take a moment to discuss what you'd like to learn about yourself today, or you can simply ask for whatever serves your highest good.

[pause]

When you're ready, take your guide by the hand. There's a doorway on the other side of the Waiting Room. Go toward that door and open it, stepping inside another delightful space. Notice that in this new space, you feel comforted and relaxed, totally safe and secure. Your guide is bringing you a screen and puts it in front of you. Notice what kind of screen it is—a television? A movie screen, a phone, a tablet, or more of a projector? Notice what you notice and know any screen is okay. Very nice.

Imagine this space has very comfortable seating. Take a seat and relax. In just a moment, your guide will play a movie that you can watch that will provide details about your past lives. Ready?

Imagine your loving guide is turning on this movie. Watch the movie now and notice what you see. What's happening? As you experience the energy of the people in this movie, are you in the movie? Who were you? What were you doing? What year is this? What part of the world are you in, or are you in another world? Very nice. Continue watching the movie. Notice what you notice.

[pause]

What's happening now? As you experience the energy of other people in the movie, is there anybody who feels like somebody you know in your current lifetime? Continue watching for as long as you're guided.

[**pause**]

Ask your guide any questions you have about what you've seen on the journey. What did they tell you? How does that affect your soul's journey? What lessons did you learn there? Why is that information important at this current time in your life?

[**pause**]

When you're ready, imagine your guide is turning off the video and putting the screen away. Take your guide by the hand and go back through the door into your Waiting Room. Thank your guide for assisting you today. Say goodbye and go back out to where you started. In a moment, when I count back from three, you will return feeling awake, refreshed, and better than you felt when you began. Three, grounded, centered, and balanced; two, processing these details in your dreams tonight, so by tomorrow morning you will be fully integrated into this new energy and information; and one, you're back!

***

How did that go? Be sure to take notes on anything important. I've always found it's incredible to go to the place in the Mindstream where these videos exist. They give you new options for accessing deep information about your soul.

BOOK OF LIFE

Earlier we discussed the widespread belief in a Book of Life that records names of souls destined for heaven. This next journey is a play on words of sorts where you will experience your own Book of Life that contains information about your prior incarnations.

Exercise

Sit down, relax, and breathe. Close your eyes. Draw the Astral Light from the universe down through the crown of your head, through your arms, fingers, torso, legs, and into your feet to connect yourself with planet earth. Surround yourself with protective golden light. Notice the door leading to your Waiting Room. Step inside now and greet your guide. Let them know what you'd like to work on today, that you'd like to take a peek at your personal Book of Life. Take your time to give and receive any necessary information before you begin the journey to set your intention.

[pause]

When you're ready, your guide will ask you to accompany them to the other side of your Waiting Room where you will find a short flight of stairs to a higher level. Take your guide by the hand and the two of you will walk up those steps now. Ready? One, two, three, walking steadily up those stairs, four, five, six, noticing that with each step you ascend, you become more relaxed and at ease. Seven, eight, you're relaxed and at peace, nine and ten. You're there now at the top of the stairs. When you gaze out, you see you're in a cozy library filled with books and comfortable seating. Imagine you and your guide can move through this room and you can take a seat. Sit there and feel the brilliantly peaceful energy of this library. Watch while your helpful guide goes about the library and returns to you carrying an old, thick book. Your guide hands this book to you now. Feel it in your hands. How does it feel? What does it look like? What is your guide telling you about this material?

Know that before opening this book in a moment, all the lifetimes that your soul ever are had inside. When you're ready, open the book and turn the pages until you arrive at the earliest lifetime you can access at this moment in your soul's history. Do that now and notice what you see. What time period is this? Who were you? Imagine that you can flip through this book, read the material, or ask your guide for details. Whenever you're ready, know you can continue moving through the many chapters so you can read more about your past lives. Take your time. Allow your higher self to easily access those past experiences that would be most for your highest good.

[**pause**]

When you're ready, close the book and allow your guide to put it away. Know that at a future time, you may come here again to gain further information that will always be for your highest good. After a moment, your guide returns from putting your Book of Life away. Take your guide's hand and walk or float toward the stairs. In a moment, you will go back down the steps and return to your Waiting Room. Ready? Ten, nine, eight, so relaxed and refreshed, seven, six, five, bringing this light and information with you now, four, three, two, one, and you're back in your Waiting Room. Be there now and thank your guide for assisting you with accessing this information. Take a moment to get any further clarification you may need about what you read today.

[**pause**]

When you feel ready, say goodbye and leave through the door to return to where you began. In a moment when I count back from three, you will regain full waking consciousness, feeling better than ever before. Three, grounded, centered, and balanced; two, processing all of this amazing information in your dreams tonight and awaking tomorrow morning feeling more refreshed than ever before; and one, you're back!

***

Did you enjoy your journey to the cozy library? Were you surprised by what you read in your Book of Life? Were these new details, or different? How do you like this kind of journey compared to some of the others we've done together?

THREAD IN TIME

Next, you're going to go on a journey I use most often when reading the Akashic Records for my clients because it easily helps access people's past lives. The great news is that by using this journey, you can do this for yourself. As usual, you'll start out in your Waiting Room, meet your guide, and go from there. Be sure to set some kind of intention in advance. Are you ready to discover some of your past lives? Good. Let's do this!

Exercise

Go ahead and sit in a comfortable chair with your hands in your lap and your feet flat on the floor. Close your eyes. Breathe. Breathe in love and peace and joy. Exhale any tensions and concerns. Very nice. Continue to breathe in through your nose, allowing your body to fully relax. Know that with each breath you take, you're becoming more and more relaxed and more and more at ease.

Bring the Astral Light through the top of your head. Feel that loving light as it moves down, down, down through the top of your head, moving into your forehead, into your eyes, your nose, your ears and jaw. Allow the loving light to move down each vertebrae of your neck, into your shoulders and the light flows down, down, down, through your arms, into your elbows, your wrists, your hands, your fingers.

Allow the light to continue moving down into your shoulders and shoulder blades, into your heart center, your stomach. Breathe loving light into your lungs, breathing in more peace and love, and exhaling any tension. Allow the healing light to move down, down, down your spine, and into your legs, your thighs, knees, ankles, and all the way down into the soles of your feet. Imagine the light is like a cord that connects you with the center of the earth. Feel the connection to earth and the connection to the universe. You are at that center. Nice job!

The light is getting stronger now, so strong it pours from your heart center establishing a beautiful golden ball of light that surrounds your body by about three feet in all directions. Feel yourself bathing in this warm, golden healing light. Know that within this loving light, you are safe, secure, and totally carefree. Only that which is of your highest good can come through.

Now notice a doorway in front of you. Open that door now. Find yourself inside your Waiting Room. Feel the loving vibrations of this special space where your soul feels totally safe, secure, and carefree. Notice what you see and hear, and how relaxed and at ease you feel here. Very good! Imagine that you can bathe in this helpful energy in your sacred space. If you have any residual tensions, let those go now. As you do, you'll notice that your beautiful guide floats down from above and joins you here. Welcome your helpful guide. Know that they are here to assist you in uncovering and accessing the information you've come here today to see, feel, or experience. Let your guide know what you'd like to work on today.

Notice now on the other side of this room is a doorway. Take your guide by the hand and the two of you will begin now to walk or float over to that door. Behind this door is a space where you and your guide will go to access important information about your past lives. In a moment when I count to three, you will open the door. Ready? One, two, three, you and your guide are opening the door. Look inside. Notice a loving, healing light is there, beckoning to you. Imagine within this loving light that a bright white strand or cord of light begins right where you're standing and moves off into the distance for as far as the eye can see. Imagine that this thread of light represents your soul's history. You're standing at a space that represents right now. In a moment, you're going to hang on to that cord of light and go all the way into the past knowing that the farther you go, the earlier the time will be. Imagine now you can set your intentions for what you would like to experience. Do you want what is for your highest good, or would you prefer something specific? Take a moment to let your loving guide know what you're inquiring about today.

[**pause**]

Take your guide by the hand and imagine the two of you can float back in time, holding on to that thread as you float all the way to an early time in your soul's history that will give you the best insights. Floating back, back, back, go way back, to the earliest moment in your soul journey that relates to what you want to know. In a moment when I count to three, you will arrive at this earliest event. Ready? One, two, and three, you're there. Be there now and notice what's happening. What year is this? Note the first thing that comes to your mind? Where are you? Take your time to notice what you notice. How do you feel? What's happening? Allow your guide to help you assimilate the information and take your time.

[pause]

When you're ready, imagine you and your guide take hold of that thread of light and begin to move forward in time. Imagine you can stop at another place in between that very early time and the present moment that will best serve your highest good and will relate to what you've come here to discover. Ready? One, floating forward in time; two, further and further, you're almost there; and three. Be there now. Notice what's happening. Where are you now? What year is this? Take your time to discover what you need to learn. Very nice!

[pause]

Now find that cord of light once again. You and your guide will hang on and move forward in time, very quickly now, coming all the way back to today. On the count of three, you'll be back at the beginning of your thread again and in the present moment. Ready? One, floating toward today; two, peaceful and relaxed; and three, you're there. Be there now, in the present moment. Open the door and float into your Waiting Room where you started. Close the door behind you. Take a moment and ask your guide questions. Why did these places or events emerge? What lessons did your soul learn? How do they apply to your current life?

[pause]

Very nice! Thank your guide for assisting you today. Imagine they will float away. Turn and walk through the door where you began. Close that door behind you. Be in the place where you started today; in a moment, when I count from five, you'll come back into the room feeling wide awake, refreshed, and better than before. Ready? Five, grounded, centered, and balanced; four, processing this information and energy in your dreams tonight so by tomorrow morning, you will be fully integrated into this new energy and information; three, driving and being safe in every activity; two, grounded, centered, and balanced; and one, you're back!

***

What past lives did you uncover with this process? Were these lives you've known about before, or did you find new information? How will these insights help you answer the question you had when you began the journey?

SUMMING UP

I hope you enjoyed taking a look at your past lives using some different techniques. As with all the journeys in the book, I know there will be some you like better than others. I encourage you to continue on with the ones that resonate best and give you the most meaningful results. At the end of the day, enjoying your journey is truly important.

Chapter Ten

FUTURE AKASHIC RECORDS IN THE FIELD OF POSSIBILITIES

Tapping into future events can be truly illuminating as you walk the path of life. Because all time is now, you can access Akashic Records that contain all future possibilities. At the same time, I would take much of the information we're about to explore with a grain of salt because the future always exists in a flexible space in the quantum field. At any given moment, the Akashic Records you witness could vary. If you see pleasant things, hold on to hope of that brighter reality. If you experience more dire conditions, know that we can all use our own free will and consciousness to shift possibilities into the loving vibrations we want to see in the world. In fact, that's what some scholars say is the real reason for doing predictive or future glimpsing work at all—the hope that something can be done about certain events to make things better. Take heart in that, always maintain optimism and hope, and continue to hold eager anticipation for the loving utopia we all want to experience. Working to better our world can make changes in the Akashic Records that will ripple through all time.

Years ago, I conducted an experiment to assist clients in creating the life of their dreams. After taking clients on typical past-life regressions, I progressed them out to their current life future to a space where they felt happy, healthy, and were successfully living out their highest potential. In this exciting future memory, whatever issues they'd been working on during our session were completely resolved. This process presupposed that because the client now had the wisdom of their future self to draw upon, they could easily point out the exact steps they took to achieve the life of their dreams. Whether the physics theories can ever be proven using our traditional scientific method, I know for sure that clients can access their futures as easily as any other part of the Mindstream.

Unrealized potential realities exist in the multiverse, and it is through guided journeys and inner work that we can view them and receive guidance on our future courses of action. By taking clients to their future happy place where their life is wonderful, people become empowered by their own inner vision to move toward the reality they truly want to create for their current lifetime. No doubt, that amazing future exists in the field of unlimited possibilities as sure as any other, so why focus on the negative when we can look to something better? The future is up for grabs, and anything is possible! In this chapter, you will explore bright potential futures in your current life and try your hand at projecting your consciousness into future realities to glimpse what's in store for humanity.

CURRENT LIFE FUTURE MEMORY JOURNEY

In this first exercise, you will acknowledge your soul purpose and go to a place in your future where you have succeeded in following your higher calling in life. The Mindstream and Akashic Records hold all possibilities that exist so, in this journey, you will access the memory or record for one of the possibilities for living at your highest level.

Exercise

Sit comfortably and gently close your eyes. Connect with the familiar Astral Light coming down through the top of your head. The light is relaxing you and healing you and carrying away all the tension from today as it continues to move down, down, down through your body and moves out the soles of your feet and into the earth, where it is transformed into healing light energy for planet Earth. Experience yourself in the center of earth and sky and create a beautiful golden ball of light that surrounds you. Notice the doorway into your Waiting Room. Open the door, step inside, and meet your guide. Let your guide know that you would like to visit your current life future and experience yourself successfully living your soul's purpose. Take a moment and discuss this with your guide.

[**pause**]

When you're ready, take your guide by the hand and move toward a doorway of your guide's choosing. Surrounded by protective light, open the door and find yourself inside a beautiful place in nature. It may be the place you've been to before, or it may be new. Either way, notice what you notice and feel how relaxing and safe you are in this special place.

Now imagine feeling lighter than you've ever felt before, so light that you and your guide begin to lift up into the air. The two of you are floating up and into the clouds, floating away, higher and higher, up, up, up, knowing that the higher up you float, the more relaxed you feel. Very good.

Now imagine you have floated so high in the sky, that as you look down, you notice something that looks or feels like a rushing river of light. That light is the Mindstream and represents how your soul experiences time. You and your guide are now floating over today. Imagine your guide can remind you of your soul's purpose, your life mission, and the reason why you incarnated at this time. Your guide can tell you, show you, or you may have an inner feeling about your purpose.

[**pause**]

Spend a moment thinking about all the ways you have already been living that purpose—lessons you learned, people you met, places you've been, all leading you to this moment. Very good.

Now imagine you can turn and look toward your future, noticing how bright the future is. In just a moment, you and your guide will travel into your current life future to an unspecified moment in your future where you are happy, healthy, and successful; it is a place where you can experience yourself successfully and happily living your soul's purpose. Ready? Let's go there now.

Take your guide by the hand and the two of you begin to float, out, out, out, over that future, further and further, into the future in your current lifetime to a place where you are happy, healthy, and living your purpose. On the count of three, you will arrive at that special place in your future. One, moving out; two, further and further; and three, you're there.

Float down, down, down, into that future event and imagine you can notice what's happening. What year is this? Notice the first thing that comes to your mind. Where are you? Again, notice the first thing that comes into your mind. What's happening? How do you feel? How does it feel to be successful and happy, knowing you are fulfilling your mission here on Earth? Take a moment to experience all you can and while you do that, go ahead and imagine you can easily remember all the steps it took you to arrive at this incredible time in your life. Notice how easy it is to remember how you got here because you've already done it.

[**pause**]

What was the first thing you did to get to this moment? And then what did you do?

And what happened next? Notice how easy it is to recall the steps you took to get to this successful place you're now in. I want you to really tune in now to the feeling of what it feels like to be so happy and successful, to know that everything has worked out even better than you could have ever imagined.

[**pause**]

When you're ready, bring those amazing feelings with you as you and your guide float all the way back to the present day again. Floating over the Mindstream, hold your guide's hand and float down, down, down, back through the clouds. Return to the lovely place in nature. Find the door to your Waiting Room and walk through that door now. Thank your guide and receive any further clarification on your experience.

[**pause**]

When you're ready, go through the door and leave your Waiting Room. Go back to where you began. In a moment when I count back from three, you will return feeling awake, refreshed, and better than you felt before. Ready? Three, grounded, centered, and balanced; two, processing the information in your dreams knowing that tomorrow you will be fully prepared to move into your brightest future; and one, you're back!

***

What did you discover when you visited your future? Were you surprised? How can you move forward in the path of the best and brightest possibility? Know that the things you experienced in that future memory are as real as you believe. For best results, follow your advice—what can you do now to move in that direction? Take some notes, then take action to see what happens.

FORK IN THE ROAD

The key to achieving greater happiness in our lives revolves around the choices we make. These possibilities are all a part of the Akashic Records. The older I get, the more time I take to make decisions because I am now more fully aware of the consequences of my decisions and how they might affect life down the road. Later, you'll have a chance to go back in time to a moment in your past when you made an important decision. For now in this next exercise, you will be able to go into the future to experience the ramifications of a decision you haven't had to make just yet.

One of the biggest reasons anyone seeks intuitive advice is because of decisions that must be made and the lack of clarity about choices and options. There's no doubt that receiving advice or a professional reading can be helpful at times, but in reality you can tap into your own higher self and find the answers to the questions you have about which direction to go in a way that I've found is far more empowering than relying on outside sources. This entire book has the tools you can use to experience those answers firsthand in a way that will make your discoveries and choices more meaningful to you because you figured these things out on your own.

Before you can begin, you'll definitely need to decide what issue you need clarity on so you can travel into the future fork in the road where you make that decision. For example, should you move to a new city or stay where you are, or is it a good idea to get married to the person you're dating or should you just stay friends? You may also want to know what the future looks like if you do stay with your current partner or if it would be better to move on alone or with someone else. Perhaps you just received a couple of amazing job offers and can't figure out which one to take. The possibilities are endless. Every day of our lives, we're faced with daunting decisions; at times, we need a little help figuring out which way to go. If any of these kinds of scenarios has ever come up for you, the following exercise is for you.

Exercise

Find your comfortable and nurturing space where you won't be disturbed. Take a moment to close your eyes, breathe, and simply be. Feel your breath moving in and out of the body and relax. Connect with the lovely Astral Light and allow that light to flow from your head to your feet as you connect with the earth. When you're ready, allow the golden light to surround you in a loving embrace. See your Waiting Room door and open it to meet your guide. Let your guide know you have a challenging decision point coming up and would like some clarity.

Take your guide's hand and walk through the door outside into nature. Feeling light as a feather, float away with your guide in your golden light bubble. Soar up into the clouds. Notice the rushing river of the Mindstream below you and know you're in the present moment. Gaze out in the direction of your current life future. This time as you do, you see a huge fork in the road ahead.

The Mindstream splits into two. Allow yourself to notice that one path represents choice A and the other path represents choice B. If you need to ask your guide for clarification about this, do so now.

[pause]

As you examine this fork in the Mindstream, I want you to immediately notice which one of these paths looks, feels, or sounds lighter or brighter to you. Allow the first thought you have to pop into your mind. Which is it—choice A or choice B? How does that realization make you feel?

In just a moment, you and your guide will float out over the Mindstream into the possible future that represents the lighter or brighter choice. You will go to a moment in your future that will be most for your highest good and give you the best sense of why this choice is right for you. Ready? One, you're floating out over the Mindstream; two, further and further; and three, you're there. Be there now! Float into this future event. Notice what's happening. What year is this, according to the first thought that comes into your mind? Where are you? What are you doing? How do you feel? How did your decision affect your life? Imagine you can know all the steps that brought you to this moment. Receive any other information you need to know.

[pause]

When you're ready, take your guide by the hand and float all the way back down the Mindstream so you're once again floating over today. Be there now and float back through the clouds, down, down, down, and land once more in the beautiful place in nature. Walk through the door into your Waiting Room. Take a moment to ask your guide for any further insights or clarification on your journey today.

[**pause**]

Thank your guide and walk through the door and go back to where you began. On the count of three, you will return feeling better than ever before. Three, processing this information in your dreams so by tomorrow you will be fully prepared to move into your best possible future; two, grounded, centered, and balanced; and one, you're back!

***

How empowering did it feel to hold your fate and future in your hands? I am so convinced that we have everything we need within us; for me, this exercise helps bring that point home. As usual, consider writing about your experiences in your journal because that information can prove invaluable as you navigate through the various crossroads of life. Later in the book, we will do the opposite and go into an event in the past that's already happened where you made a choice and do some healing that I think you'll find incredibly enlightening.

SYMBOL FOR SUCCESS

Your higher self dictates what you experience during any guided journey. Moving into the space of happiness to events that have not yet occurred is like tapping into pure potentiality and experiencing firsthand the desired influences you want to feel so you can hopefully bring those sensations back to the present moment and create your preferred outcome. To deepen your sense of your best possible future, you can identify a symbol within the

Akashic Records that signals your higher self to shoot for success. The symbol may be an image from your past lives or something your soul has encountered in your current lifetime. It might be something you've never thought of before. Regardless of the symbol that emerges, the purpose of the image is to assist you in tuning in so you can consciously hang onto that image and refer to that symbol down the road to give you signs and clues that what you're doing is right on track.

The next exercise will help you tune into the future and find your own symbol so you'll know when your otherworldly helpers and guides are attempting to give you love and support. Remember, the symbol is designed to help you bring something back from the future to use in the present. Life can be challenging. We can all use as many resources as possible to make sense of our lives. I know from personal experience and from watching my clients that having a symbol for success really works. Ready? Let's begin!

Exercise

Sit comfortably, close your eyes, and relax. Bring the loving Astral Light from head to feet connecting you with earth and sky. The golden protective bubble of light surrounds you, and you easily find your doorway to your Waiting Room. Step inside and greet your guide. Share your intentions to find a symbol to help you on your life path. Take your guide by the hand and return through the doorway into the place in nature you visited before. The moment you arrive there, you're feeling so light and refreshed, the two of you float away into the clouds.

Find yourselves back above the Mindstream, a rushing river of light. Gaze in the direction of your current life's future. The moment you do, you and your guide begin to float to a moment in your current life future where you're happy and healthy and succeeding at manifesting your life's purpose. This could be an event you've seen before, or it might be new. When I count to three, you will arrive. One, moving out into your future; two, further and further, you're almost there; and three, you're there! Be there now. Notice what's happening. What year is this? What are you doing to create joy and happiness in your life? Feel those feelings of joy and peace. Now imagine your subconscious mind and higher self can give you a symbol—a thought or a special visual image—that represents the feeling of joy you're having. It could be a flower, a butterfly, or anything you want, just notice that symbol, allowing the first thing you think of to pop into your mind. What is your symbol? What does your symbol represent? If you need clarity, ask your guide to help you understand your symbol.

[pause]

Good job! Know that anytime you see this symbol out in the physical world, such as on TV, a billboard, or on the internet, or when it floats into your mind, you will be instantly drawn back to the feeling of success and joy that you're now experiencing. Whenever you consciously think of this symbol, you will easily recall your future success and you will feel a deep sense of joy and happiness. Take those amazing feelings with you now as you and your guide float back toward the present, toward today, but only as quickly as you can allow all the feelings of peace and success to fill your entire being. In a moment when I count to three, you will once again be floating over today. One, two, and three, you're there floating over today.

Take your guide's hand and float down, down, down, back through the clouds, until you once again find yourself landing where you started inside your beautiful place in nature. Open the door and return to your Waiting Room. Be there now. Thank your guide and ask for any further clarification. When you're ready, say goodbye and go through the door you first entered. You are still surrounded by a golden ball of light—safe, secure, and totally carefree, knowing you can keep this light with you always and that within the light, only that which is of your highest good comes through. Take all the energy you need to feel awake, refreshed, and better than before, but send any excess energy down, down, down, through your legs, and out the soles of your feet, down into the earth. You are grounded, centered and balanced. In a moment when I count back from five, you will return to waking consciousness feeling refreshed and better than you did before. Five, grounded, centered, and balanced; four, continuing to process this information in your dreams tonight so by tomorrow morning, you will be fully integrated into this new energy; three, driving safely and being safe in all activities; two, grounded, centered, and balanced; and one, you're back!

***

Take a moment to either draw or write down a description of your new symbol in your journal so you can start being on the lookout for it. You may also want to do an online search for images that remind you of the symbol, or perhaps even search through emojis in your phone. No doubt, our society is moving into a new consciousness where symbols are more important than ever. In this case, know when your symbol shows up in your mind or in the outer world, you can rest assured you're receiving a positive sign of good things to come.

FUTURE BOOK OF LIFE

Earlier in the section on past lives, you had a chance to go to a cozy library and read from your Book of Life. The spiritual philosophy behind such a book includes the idea that you should not only be able to access your past lives from it but your future lives as well. Next, you will return to that library where your guide took you before, only this time you will access your Book of Life and see what kinds of future lives you have to look forward to on your soul's journey.

Exercise

Close your eyes, breathe, and draw down the Astral Light through your body. Stand between heaven and earth and surround yourself with your golden healing bubble of light. Walk through the door that leads to your Waiting Room now. Your guide greets you. Let them know that today you'd like to view chapters in your personal Book of Life that relate to lifetimes you're going to have after your current life. Take your time to give and receive any necessary information before you begin.

[**pause**]

When you're ready, your guide will ask you to accompany them to the other side of your Waiting Room where you will find a short flight of stairs leading to a higher level. Take your guide by the hand, and the two of you will walk up those steps now. Ready? One, two, three, walking steadily up those stairs, four, five, six, noticing that with each step you ascend, you become more relaxed and at ease. Seven, eight, you're relaxed and at peace, nine and ten. You're there now at the top of the stairs. Find yourself back inside your cozy library filled with books and comfortable seating.

Go ahead and have a seat. You might choose to sit where you sat before, or you may find your guide wants to direct you to a new part of this library. Either way, go with your guide and find a place where you will feel completely comfortable. Sit there and feel the peaceful and loving energy of this library. Watch while your helpful guide goes about the library and returns to you carrying a thick book. This may be the same book you saw before, or it might be new. Either way, know that within this book are the records for your future self, of lives you will experience in the future of your soul's progression through time. Your guide hands this book to you now. Hold it in your hands. How does it feel? What does it look like? What is your guide telling you about this material?

[pause]

Know that in a moment when you open this book, you will find details of all future lifetimes your soul will experience. When you're ready, open the book to a random page and access details about your future. What time period is this? Are you still on Earth or another planet? What's happening? Imagine that you can flip through this book, read the material, ask your guide for details, or simply have a feeling about what the book contains. Take your time. Allow your higher self to easily access experiences that would be most for your highest good.

[pause]

Take a moment to ask your guide some important questions. Why is this future material important for you to know right now? How do your future activities relate to your soul's purpose? What benefit will this information bring you? When you're ready, close the book and watch while your guide takes it back where it belongs. After a moment, your guide returns. Take your guide's hand and walk or float back toward the stairs. In a moment, you will go back down the steps and return to your Waiting Room. Ready? Ten, nine, eight, so relaxed and refreshed, seven, six, five, bringing this light and information with you now, four, three, two, one, and you're back in your Waiting Room. Be there now and thank your guide for assisting you. Take a moment to receive further clarification about what you read today.

[**pause**]

When you feel ready, say goodbye and leave through the door and return to where you began. In a moment when I count back from three, you will return to full waking consciousness, feeling better than ever before. Three, grounded, centered, and balanced; two, processing all of this amazing information in your dreams tonight and awaking tomorrow morning feeling more refreshed than ever before; and one, you're back!

***

How did you do accessing your future lives? Were you surprised by what you read in your future Book of Life? How will you use this information to your advantage moving forward?

PREDICTIVE JOURNEY TO THE FUTURE
There's no doubt that Nostradamus and other historical figures mentioned earlier in the book must have somehow accessed the Akashic Records that specifically relate to future events. Far-flung distance predictions are never taken seriously at the time the forecasts are made but gain wider attention in hindsight. Nostradamus's quatrains are a good example because they were so vague;

modern seekers have a pretty easy time prescribing those items to global events. Edgar Cayce made some correct predictions but many didn't happen at all. Thanks to the ever- changing interplay of space, time, and matter, future events are in flux and subject to change. This next exercise will give you a chance to peek into the future of planet Earth. Realize that you may not be able to get anything from this kind of inquiry if it's not meant for you to know, an idea that holds true for all parts of the Akashic Records. I specialize in past lives, for example, but other kinds of information would never emerge for me at all. If you're curious, feel free to give this a try and see what happens.

Exercise

Sit in your comfortable space and close your eyes. Breathe and relax and allow the Astral Light to move from head to toe. Surround yourself with the golden protective light, and enter your Waiting Room. Discuss future possibilities with your guide. Let them know that you would like to go into a space that would allow you to glimpse Earth's future. Take a moment to discuss this intention and see what your guide has to say. If you'd like, you may ask your guide for permission to proceed and whether or not this information is possible for you to know.

[pause]

If your guide agrees and once you're both ready, take your guide by the hand and walk or float toward a door on the other side of your Waiting Room. Open that door and find yourself inside a metallic, high frequency room. Feel the incredibly high vibrations of this space and move through that area until you find yourself at a table with a couple of chairs. Sit with your guide at the table. Notice there's a huge glass or crystal ball on that table. When you're ready, images of events that have not happened yet will begin to float within that crystal ball. Take your time to notice what you notice, see what you see, and feel what you feel.

[pause]

When you've seen all that you can today, the images slow to a stop. Ask your guide for specific details or to provide any information about what you saw in the crystal. What year or years were you looking at? What was happening? How can this information make an impact on your current life behavior? What would humanity need to change to prevent unwanted influences from changing it, or what would you need to continue doing to ensure the best possible future outcome?

[pause]

When all your have been questions answered, stand up and walk or float with your guide through this amazing space and return through the door to your Waiting Room. Be there now. Thank your guide and allow them to share any further details.

[pause]

When you're ready, say goodbye for now and leave your Waiting Room. Go back to where you began. Be there now. When I count back from three, you will return. Three, bringing all your focus and awareness back to your present life and experience; two, grounded, centered, and balanced; and one, you're back!

***

How did that go? Were you able to receive any information? How do you feel about it? What do you believe is the likelihood that this information may or may not come to pass? The purpose for prophecies and predictions is to help positive outcomes happen and to avoid calamities. Did you receive any wisdom about what could be done to create a bright future?

SUMMING UP

Remember my advice at the beginning of this chapter to take future journey work for what it is—a possibility. If you enjoyed your visions, wonderful. If you found much to be desired, then think of how certain realities may be avoided through your mind power and free will. The future is up for grabs and better days are on the horizon if we keep the faith.

Chapter Eleven

PARALLEL UNIVERSES AND CONSCIOUSNESS EXPANSION

After years of my own personal self-reflection and the tremendous privilege of working with thousands of people from all walks of life around the world, I've come to understand that past-life regression, future memory journeys, trips to meet with lost loved ones, or finding the soul's purpose are all examples of parallel universes and the multiverse at work, and Akashic Records can be accessed in all of these areas. Ever since Sir Thomas Young conducted his famous slit experiment in 1801 that proved light can exist in more than one place at the same time, quantum physicists insist that the same holds true for you and me. I've certainly witnessed that concept firsthand through the spiritual epiphanies of my clients and readers. In this chapter, you will have a chance to consciously visit parallel universes and alternative realities, and explore your connection to the universe. Enjoy!

PARALLEL UNIVERSE JOURNEY

In the early 2000s, I had a dream that forever changed the course of my life. In it, a dear friend and I rode in the backseat of a taxi down a two-lane highway in a gorgeous mountainous oceanic environment I had never seen before. I gazed out the windows of the cab and saw mountains on one side, the ocean on the other. At some point, I separated from my friend and wound up in a small town where I experienced vivid details about my job and friendship with several coworkers. Unlike most dreams that vanish from our minds the moment we wake up, this one stuck with me. I called my friend to tell him about it but before I could finish, he started describing the same place I'd seen and told me *he was there*! Like many of my book projects that begin seemingly by accident, I asked my friend, "Do you think we're living in a parallel universe together?" That question led me to conduct several interesting experiments over the next few years where clients accessed information that led them to believe that they existed in more than one dimension of reality. Clients realized that our souls can actually experience the same lessons and learnings in many dimensions. Next, you'll get to experience the same journey I took those clients on and discover for yourself whether or not you exist in parallel universes by connecting with universal consciousness and an incredibly high frequency healing light that can be quite transformational. You can set specific intentions to find out if you have the same purpose throughout the multiverse, or you could simply ask for your highest good.

Exercise

Sit down and close your eyes. Draw the Astral Light of source down through the top of your head and feel that loving light pouring through your body, into every cell as it moves through the soles of your feet, connecting you with the core of the earth. Surround yourself with a protective golden light, knowing that only that which is of highest good can come through, and walk through the door of your Waiting Room.

Your guide is waiting for you. Say hello and discuss any intentions you'd like to set before traveling into a space where you can experience yourself in multiple universes.

[pause]

Taking your guide by the hand, the two of you will walk through the door and outside into nature. The moment you arrive, you begin to float. Feel yourself lifting up, up, up, off of the ground, floating higher, and higher and higher. You're floating up through the clouds. Continue to float up, up, up, higher and higher and higher with your guide by your side. Know that that the higher up you float, the more relaxed you feel. Floating freely now in outer space, feel the expansive energy of the universe and know that all is well. Peaceful and relaxed, you have now floated so high in the sky, you notice a doorway in front of you floating in the stars. Float up to that door with your guide and imagine you can open the door. Inside that door is the highest frequency light you've ever seen. Go with your guide and float through the doorway now, and find yourself inside this space filled with high frequency pure white light. The frequency of the light is so transformational and healing, you're instantly filled with peace and joy. The peaceful feeling is so powerful, you instantly become twice as relaxed as you were before you arrived, and you feel more relaxed and at ease than you have ever been before. Very good!

As you begin to look around the room, you can feel the incredible energy and may hear sounds as your body continues to absorb this peaceful light. On the other side of the room, you notice a doorway. The door is opening now, and out walks the most beautiful being you have ever seen. This light-filled presence moves slowly toward you, and you notice the being is filled with pure love and light and the knowingness of the entire universe. This omnipotent presence represents the All That Is. The cosmic awareness of everything in the entire universe is embodied within the consciousness of this amazing being. Because of that, you realize the being knows every single thing there is to know about you, your soul, and your soul's journey, as well as everything in the universe that has ever been or ever will be in the future.

And as you bathe in the unconditional love and beautiful feelings the being has for you, you realize you have come here today to ask this special being a very important question: "Am I currently living in parallel universes or alternative realities, yes or no?" Immediately notice the first answer that pops into your mind. Very good! If the answer is no, thank the being and continue to bask in this celestial light for as long as you would like. You may then ask the loving being for any important information that would serve your highest good at this time. You may ask what your soul's purpose is, or how you may best fulfill your current life mission; anything you'd like to know. Take your time, then thank the being and end your journey there.

If the answer is yes, you can ask, "How many universes?" Notice the first number that pops into your mind. Very good!

Imagine that the being steps aside and three paths of light appear directly behind them. Very good! These paths represent other dimensions where you're currently residing. Imagine now you can notice which of the three paths looks or feels the lightest or brightest. Good! Now walk or float over to the lightest or brightest path. This path represents the road into a parallel universe where you currently reside, a universe that will be most for your highest good that will give you the most insights into your soul's purpose. In a moment when I count to three, you and your personal guide will step on the path and be transferred to this alternative reality. The path is like a moving walkway so it goes very, very quickly. Ready? One, two, three, you and your guide are stepping on the path now. Feel yourself moving very quickly—zip, zip, zip, moving very quickly out, out, out—by the time I count to three, you will arrive at your destination. One, floating out, out, out, two; further and further; you're almost there, and three, you're there. You and your guide feel yourselves stopping.

Be there now, look around and notice what you see or feel. What year is this, the first thing that comes into your mind? Where are you in the world, or are you in another world? How do you feel? Imagine you can look down at your feet and notice what kind of shoes you're wearing, if any. Good! As you experience your soul in this space, what is your purpose? Notice the first thing that comes to your mind. How does this mission or purpose relate to the life you're currently living? Take your time to understand anything you need to know.

[**pause**]

When you're ready, turn around and notice the path of light again. In just a moment, you and your guide will step on that path and return to where you came from. Ready? One, two, three, go with your guide and step on the path and go back, back, back, and arrive in the light-filled room with the being where you started. Be there now and imagine you are once again with the beautiful being of light. Imagine walking or floating up to this loving being once again and feel the love and high regard the being has for you.

Imagine that in the presence of such high-level intelligence you have the opportunity to ask the being about anything you want to know. This being knows everything about everything, so you can ask those questions now. You may want to know, "What is the meaning of life?" or "What is the secret of the universe?" or "Why are we here?" Take a moment to receive answers to your questions.

[pause]

Very good! Now imagine that you can thank the being, and notice the being floats back through the door where it came from. Once again, you are in the room of peaceful light and you turn your attention to your guide. Take your guide by the hand and begin to walk or float toward the door you came through. Open the door now and find yourself out in space once again. You and your guide are floating down, down, down, through the stars and clouds, and down, down, down, feeling the forces of gravity pulling you back to the earth until once again, you land in the beautiful place in nature. Walk toward the door and return to your Waiting Room. Thank your guide for assisting you, and if you have more questions, take your time to receive that information now.

[pause]

When you're ready, turn and exit the door of your Waiting Room and return to where you first started. You are still surrounded by a golden ball of light, knowing that within the golden ball only that which is of your highest good can come through. Imagine you can take all of the energy you need to feel awake and refreshed but that any excess energy will begin now to float down, down, down, through your legs and out the soles of your feet. That excess energy is going down into the earth. Imagine you are sending this excess healing energy into the earth and you are now completely grounded, centered, and balanced. In a moment when I count from five, you will return, feeling awake, refreshed, and better than you did before. Five, grounded, centered, and balanced; four, continuing to process this information in your dream state so by tomorrow morning you will be fully integrated into this new awareness; three, driving safely and being safe in all activities; two, grounded, centered, and balanced; and one, you're back!

***

So, how do you feel? How was your journey? Interesting, wasn't it? How did your purpose transcend different dimensions? How were you affected by the healing of the high frequency light and the love of the being you met? You may want to record your experience in your journal.

CRITICAL DECISION POINT

There's not a person alive who doesn't live with at least one regret or nagging feeling about a past decision; I think it is part of human nature. We want to experience greater happiness in life, and much of our experience of satisfaction comes directly from the choices put into play in the past.

Through the lens of our own personal experience along with feedback from outside influences, we come to the best conclusion we can reason out at the time. Our decision making becomes a moment-by-moment movement in the direction our soul believes will make us happier in the long run. Quantum physicists believe that each choice we make creates a new universe. What happens eventually, though, is that no matter how good our life is going, it can't last one hundred percent of the time. Everybody alive has troubles and challenges at least every now and then. During such times, it's natural to think back to the collective steps that brought us to a particular place in life and wonder what might have been.

When working with clients, regrets and challenges are often at the forefront of people's minds. Years ago, I found a way to help people find greater peace about their decisions by asking them to return to a point in their current life when they were faced with a major decision. Once there, clients were asked to imagine making the opposite choice and progressing into their future to see what would have happened if they had made the other decision. This sounds far out, I know, but every single client who did this was able to see that their original choice was the best one. They walked away from the session feeling like they could finally let go of the nagging feeling of wondering and what-if's that are so irksome. Is that because of a subconscious need to justify one's actions? Or is it because the path they chose was truly the better path, for their highest good? More importantly, are both realities coexisting all at once in other dimensions of reality, or did they make the whole experience up? We really cannot know that with any degree of certainty. The bottom line is the clients felt better in the now, and for me, that's what matters most.

In terms of parallel worlds, I'm still left with the idea that these possibilities must be coexisting in alternate worlds as some unrealized future potential. They are part of the Mindstream and the Akashic Records, existing in eternity. In modern physics, the Everett-Wheeler Many Worlds Interpretation (MWI) suggests that each decision point sends you on to a new timeline. I certainly believe this is possible, particularly after going through my own journeys and seeing this firsthand with clients.

We all have the ability to tune in to what is for our highest and best if given the right tools. I truly hope I have provided some of those with this writing. Certainly the clients I interviewed were all able to say that had they chosen the other path, it was at best the same but never better than the one they actually selected. In many cases, the other path would have been harder, much worse, and way more undesirable. These new paths illuminated totally different lives for people in which they did not have the same spouses, children, friends, or jobs. Most clients could not even conceive of a life without their current loved ones, something that in and of itself gave rise to renewed feelings of gratitude that were perhaps lacking prior to the session. Everyone alive periodically experiences the inevitable state of apathy at one time or another. The process assisted clients in returning to their lives with renewed vigor, enthusiasm, and gratitude, having unloaded the weight of past regrets.

It's incredibly helpful to finally put certain things to rest and to come to a deep inner knowing at a more experiential level that what was done in the past really and truly worked. If our ultimate goal in life is to find greater peace and happiness and experience more love and light, the first person we should consider extending such loving grace to is *ourselves*. Nagging what-ifs keep us from self-acceptance. By putting some of those self-doubts down and letting go of regret, this next guided journey can be a real game changer. Are you ready to see for yourself? Great! Let's do this!

Exercise

Think back to a time in your life when you made a critical decision that you know beyond a shadow of a doubt affected and altered the rest of your life. I'm talking about a *big* decision such as staying where you are versus moving to a new state, marrying someone, or picking one job over another. Take your time to fully bring this memory into focus within your mind. You may also find it quite helpful to write the memory down and fully explore your feelings at the time about the conflict you may have felt and what an effect this decision would have on your future. Once that's done, you're ready to proceed.

Close your eyes and begin to relax. Take a deep, cleansing breath in through your nose, breathing in peace and relaxation, exhaling tension and concern. Connect with the Astral Light, allowing a beam of pure white light to move through the top of your head, into your forehead, your eyes, feel the light moving down, down, down into your neck and shoulders, into your elbows, wrists, hands and fingers, through your neck and shoulders, into your heart, into your stomach, down into the base of your spine, into your legs, down, down, down into the soles of your feet. Feel the light extending into the earth. Feel yourself in the center of earth and sky and know you are now connected with the All That Is. The Astral Light pours from your heart, surrounding you with a golden ball of light. You know that inside the golden ball you are safe, secure, and totally carefree.

Notice the door to your Waiting Room. Walk into the room and see your guide. Take a moment to talk to your guide and explain this decision you made in your past. Tell your loving guide all about what happened, how you felt, and any other important details. Take your time to receive any feedback your guide has for you.

[pause]

Take your guide by the hand and notice a doorway on the other side of your Waiting Room. Open that door now and find yourself inside a high frequency space filled with light. Notice you're still surrounded by that golden bubble of light. That golden ball of light begins now to carry you and your guide up, up, up. You're floating now, moving higher and higher and higher, noticing that the higher up you float, the more relaxed you feel. Continue to float up, up, up, up, up, higher and higher and higher, floating above the world and into the universe.

Notice now that you have floated so high up, you notice a bright river of light below you. That light represents time. Imagine you're floating over today, carefree and relaxed. Turn now and look back toward your past. In just a moment, I want you and your guide to float in that golden bubble of light over the past to the moments before you made that critical decision. Ready? Begin now, feel yourself moving back, back, back, further and further back in time, so on the count of three you will be floating over the moments before you made your decision. One, floating back, back, back; two, further and further; and three, you're there.

Be there now and notice you can float over that time in your life and easily recall those thoughts and memories. What year is this? What is the decision you're making? What are your options? How do you feel? Imagine you can recall all the reasons for making the decision you did at that time.

[**pause**]

Very nice. Now consider the path you did not take. As you do, I want you to notice that you're still floating over the beautiful river of light. Notice now that the river of light forks off into a new direction. That direction represents what would have happened if you had made the other choice.

Surrounded by protective light and taking your loving guide by the hand, float out over that new event. Float as far forward in time as you feel guided. As you do, notice how you feel making a different decision. Float forward in time to an unspecified moment that would best demonstrate the outcome of your new decision.

Ready? One, floating out, out, out; two, further and further; and three, you're there. Be there now and notice what's happening. What year is this, the first thing that comes to mind? How do you feel? And what's going on there? How is your life different thanks to this new decision? Take a moment for your guide to assist you in noticing all you need to know.

[pause]

When you're ready, leave this event and float back in time to the fork in the road where you were before. Notice the choice you did make and see how the line of light that represents your current lifetime is actually lighter and brighter than the option you just visited. See how your current life is a bright light stretches out into your future. Notice the choice you did not make that you visited today. Imagine that as you notice it, that light disappears into thin air. Now, the only light that remains is the one that leads you into your current life future, the path you chose so long ago. Notice as the other possibility vanishes, your life path becomes even lighter and brighter and feels even better than it ever did before. Good job! Taking your guide by the hand, the two of you will float forward in time bringing this energy and awareness with you as you return to the present moment and find yourself floating over today. Be there now. You are floating over today in your present, current lifetime and feeling better than you've ever felt before.

How do you feel now about the choice you made long ago? If there were any regrets, imagine that you can now easily release them and know you made the best choice. Notice what it feels like to no longer wonder or second guess yourself and how much lighter and brighter you feel now than when you began. Ask your guide to reinforce the realization that the path you chose long ago was best for your soul and overall happiness. Take your time and allow your guide to share helpful insights with you.

[pause]

When you're ready and still holding your guide's hand, the two of you begin to float down, down, down, through the light again until you begin feeling the gravitational forces of earth bringing you down until once again you land back where you started in the space filled with light. You notice that you are still surrounded by that loving golden light and are safe, secure, and totally protected. Walk back through the door into your Waiting Room. Close that door behind you. If you need any more information, ask your guide now.

[pause]

When you're ready, thank your guide and say goodbye. Walk through the door to your Waiting Room, closing that door behind you, and be where you started. In a moment when I count from three, you will feel wide awake, refreshed, and better than you did before. Ready? Three, you're grounded, centered, and balanced; two, you're processing this information in your dreams tonight so by tomorrow morning you will be fully integrated into the awareness that you need not regret your past. You understand now that you're living the best possible outcome for your life; one, driving safely and being safe in all activities; and you're back!

***

How did you do? Were you pleasantly surprised by what you found, or was the difference more subtle? Are you now able to move on knowing you did your best at the time? What I like best about this process is the idea that you're likely to find true experiential answers to the nagging feeling of regret. The longer I live on this earth, the more I am convinced that our past mistakes are not mistakes at all. I don't think there's a person alive who wouldn't be doing the best they can in any given moment depending on what they're facing. Sometimes you do your best and disaster follows. You may spend years with regret, but wait long enough and you may also see that those challenges made you stronger down the road—that is the true blessing you receive even in the toughest times.

Whatever information you received from this journey, I hope you can gain new perspective and come to an experiential understanding of the idea that our challenges make us who we are and help us in meaningful ways. Be sure to take notes about anything important that you discovered here. Above all, go easy on yourself and work toward accepting what happened in the past, releasing it, and moving forward while knowing you accomplished much simply through experience. To finally come to peace about painful issues in our past—particularly in our current life—and to love ourselves despite whatever happened is the greatest gift we can ever give ourselves. I want that for you!

CONSCIOUSNESS EXPANSION AND GLOBAL HEALING

We are all one, as they say, and one of my favorite ways to explore the Mindstream is connecting with other people, countries, plants, animals, and so forth by extending loving light to our planet and humanity. You can do this next exercise daily to transcend all time and connect with the entire cosmos. Global healing only takes a couple of minutes, and by repeating exercises like these often, you can easily expand your consciousness and aware-ness of all beings in the process. I hope you will enjoy this voyage. Ready?

Exercise

Sit in your sacred space. Close your eyes and breathe. Allow the Astral Light to move through your head and feet, connecting you to earth and sky. Imagine the light surrounds you in a golden, heal-ing embrace. Now notice the door to your Waiting Room. Open that door now and step inside the Waiting Room. Your guide is there to greet you. Notice a chair where you can sit. Sit down and relax as you sense the golden ball of light around you. Expand that golden ball of light and allow your light to fill the entire Waiting Room. Expand your light into the building or home where you started your journey, knowing you can touch every corner and be in all those places at once. Move outside now, out to the street where your car's parked. Move your energy into your neighbor-hood, into the city, suburb, or town where you live. Imagine you can expand your light and energy until you fill up the entire state or region where you live. Move through your country. Feel your light and consciousness stretching across the oceans and conti-nents, wrapping around the earth, surrounding the entire planet with your loving light. Send your loving, healing golden light to all people, animals, beings, countries, continents. Very nice. Now imagine yourself lifting up, up, up, leaving the earth behind as you stretch your light and energy into outer space. Imagine your-self floating up toward the moon. Place your consciousness on the moon and view Earth from the moon. How do you feel? Very good! Lift up, off of the moon, traveling further and further away from the earth. Notice the stars and galaxies as you expand and connect with the entire universe. Feel yourself sending love and light to the entire universe, and feel the unconditional love and expansion of connecting with the All That Is.

When you're ready, feel yourself moving through space, floating down, down, down, back toward the earth. Connecting with all continents and oceans, begin now to move all your light and energy to your own country, sending love to all people, animals, and living beings. Send your energy to your region, your town or city, your neighborhood, your street. Notice your energy right outside the building. Move your energy inside, into the space where you started this journey today, and finally into your Waiting Room. All your loving light is now inside your Waiting Room. Notice your guide is there with you. If you need to ask any questions, do so now.

[pause]

When you're ready, take all of the energy and light you need and get up from the chair you're sitting in inside your Waiting Room. Thank your guide. Know you will see your guide again soon. Go back out the door where you first came into the Waiting Room, closing the door behind you. You're back where you started. In a moment when I count from three, you'll return to waking consciousness feeling rested and refreshed, like you've had an energizing nap. Ready? Three, you are grounded, centered, and balanced; two, you can continue to benefit from the universal light and love feeling connected to all in the universe and remaining protected inside the golden ball of healing light; and one, you're back!

***

It's incredibly helpful to take a moment out of your busy day to send light to everyone on our own planet and in the universe at large. I always feel better when I do this and I hope you'll join me in extending your light to others whenever you have a free moment.

SUMMING UP

Time is an illusion. By tapping into the Mindstream, you can shift the way you view reality and hopefully change your life for the better while feeling the deep interconnectedness we all share as inhabitants of planet earth and the universe as a whole. I hope you enjoyed your experience of your multidimensional self!

CONCLUSION

Writing *Journeys Through the Akashic Records* and working with clients through the years has been extremely gratifying. I'm glad to be able to finally give this information to people in a format that can be hopefully used for years to come. At the same time, this work has once again left me wondering about time and life in general. More than twenty years ago, I entered my current line of work because past-life regression and energy healing made such a profound improvement in my own life in helping me deal with unresolved grief that I hoped to ultimately make some kind of impact on others. After all these years working with so many clients, you may be surprised to learn I actually have more questions about past-life regression and the nature of humanity than I did when I first began this strange career of mine.

How does this thing called life really work? I've realized that to limit myself by only defining and attributing such weirdness to past-life memories alone cannot be fully correct. There's much more to people than simple reincarnation and rebirth. How so? I'm still grappling with that question to this day. I don't believe that we beings can ever fully understand ourselves while still alive in earthly form and residing within our physical bodies. These are the questions that humankind will likely continue to wonder about forever. I've noticed over the years that readers and students have wanted me to emphatically state beyond a shadow of a doubt that I believe that past lives are real, but the reality is I cannot do that.

I don't believe anyone can say so with one hundred percent certainty. Human beings cannot grasp the vast storehouse of the universal mind.

Theories such as Jung's Collective Unconsciousness and the Akashic Records themselves theoretically debunk the concept of past lives altogether. When any idea is so pervasive that it permeates our entire culture and communities around the world, you could argue that the supposed past-life recollection is not that at all but instead an example of someone who simply (perhaps unwittingly) tapped into the Akashic Records. The idea that the Mindstream may dismiss reincarnation does not bother me in the least; I've never been concerned with attempting to prove reincarnation is real. Past-life regression as a therapy helps people because they are able to view themselves through a broader lens and release old patterns and unwanted influences in doing so. So long as a session or journey results in greater peace and happiness, my mission has been accomplished.

I am often asked amid all the complexities I explore in my books whether or not I believe in a higher intelligence or God. My answer is a resounding yes. I believe our creator developed simultaneous lives and parallel realities as part of that divine creation. Exploring the Akashic Records and Mindstream begs another question: are these places *real* even though we cannot perceive them through our primary senses? The widespread belief in Akasha is universally accepted in civilizations around the world and has been since the beginning of recorded history. That fact alone is enough evidence that I must say yes. This unseen force is likely a more accurate depiction of reality than our own three-dimensional existence.

While science has advanced tremendously over the course of modern civilization, so many mysteries remain. All belief systems and conclusions we use to define our reality here on earth, including science, were created by us and are part of that collective illusion we have agreed to participate in during our lives. To insist the scientific method is the end-all, be-all and that things must be observed to be valid while dismissing any ideas that do not fit within those stringent boundaries is ridiculous. Albert Einstein believed our current thinking must be overhauled for humanity to thrive.[8] I wholeheartedly agree.

I pray for an end to all suffering and hope that humanity can experience a total understanding of our own personal light and power so that higher ideals can become a permanent fixture in our collective consciousness. Glimpsing beyond the veil into the Akasha gives us a view of the divine light embedded in all things. With that vision, anything is possible. Far beyond our own worldly concerns, for any of us to become happier and more fulfilled in our own lives, we must pause to consider not only our own individual happiness but the light that exists in all people, nations, and beings in and around our world and the infinite realm of the Akasha. How do our actions further the positive shifts in the collective to benefit everyone? Accessing Akashic space and the Mindstream allows us to empathetically connect with our fellow beings and extend the light of compassion in a powerfully transformational way.

When we're in the midst of troubles in our lives, it's so easy to fall into despair and believe that things can't improve, but nothing could be further from the truth! We're here, alive in this moment for a reason and can endure and transcend any challenge if we put our minds to it. I hope this material has found you in just the right moment in your life to assist you with blasting through the constricting illusions of material reality to expand your consciousness

---

8. "Albert Einstein Quotes," Brainy Quote website, Accessed April 2021. https://www.brainyquote.com/quotes/albert_einstein_104567.

into the sphere of unlimited possibility. Venturing into the Mindstream is a way to experience your divinity in a meaningful way. I hope this book has given you to pause to consider the vast storehouse of data, energy, and information available to you within the Mindstream. I pray you will be able to visit these places to expand your awareness and create greater peace in your life and in the lives of those around you. I wish you peace, joy, and happiness on your path now and always. Namaste!

BIBLIOGRAPHY

"Albert Einstein Quotes." Brainy Quote website. Accessed April 22, 2021 https://www.brainyquote.com/quotes/albert_einstein_104567.

The Edgar Cayce Foundation. "Edgar Cayce Readings, 1971, 1993–2007."

Bandler, Richard, and John Grinder. *Frogs into Princes: Neuro Linguistic Programming*. Moab, UT: Real People Press, 1979.

Bible, King James Version.

Blavatsky, Helena Petrovna. *Isis Unveiled: Volumes I & II*. New York: Start Publishing, 2012. Originally published 1876 by Theosophical University Press (New York).

———. *The Secret Doctrine (Complete): The Synthesis of Science, Religion, and Philosophy, Third and Revised Edition*. Ashland, OH: Library of Alexandria Baker & Taylor, 2012. Originally published 1888 by Theosophical University Press (New York).

Gyatso, Bhiksu Tenzin, the Fourteenth Dalai Lama, and Bhiksuni Thubten Chodron. *Approaching the Buddhist Path*. Somerville, MA: Wisdom Publications, 2017.

Ianonne, A. Pablo. *Dictionary of World Philosophy*. Routledge, NY: 2001.

Jung, C. G., and Gerhard Adler. *The Collected Works of C. G. Jung, Vol. 7: Two Essays on Analytical Psychology 2nd ed*. New York: Bollingen Foundation and Princeton University Press, 1953, 1966, 1972.

Laszlo, Ervin. *Science & the Akashic Field: An Integral Theory of Everything, 2nd Edition*. Rochester, VT: Inner Traditions, 2010.

Nostradamus. *The Complete Prophecies of Nostradamus*. Radford, VA: Wilder Publications, 2007.

Singh, Ritu. "From 'Great Disasters & Cataclysms' to Cancer Cure: Here are Blind Mystic Baba Vanga's Predictions for 2021." India.com. Accessed January 2021. https://www.india .com/viral/2021-predictions-great-disasters-to-cancer -cure-here-are-blind-mystic-baba-vangas-predictions-for -2021-4289919/.

Sinnett, A. P. *Esoteric Buddhism*. New York: The Riverside Press, Houghton, Mifflin & Company, 1892.

Stefon, Matt. "Bardo Thödol." In *Encyclopedia Britannica*. Article published October 16, 2015. https://www.britannica.com /topic/Bardo-Thodol.

Steinbach, Susie. "Victorian era." In *Encyclopedia Britannica*. Article published October 2019, https://www.britannica.com /event/Victorian-era.

Steiner, Rudolf, *True Knowledge of the Christ: Theosophy and Rosicrucianism—The Gospel of John (Collected Works of Rudolf Steiner Book 100)*. Translated by Anna R. Meuss. East Sussex, UK: Rudolf Steiner Press, 2015.

Wolf, Fred Alan. *Parallel Universes: The Search for Other Worlds*. New York: Simon & Schuster, 1988.

ADDITIONAL RESOURCES

Thank you for taking this journey with me! Here are some other resources you may find helpful and interesting as you explore the Akashic Records further:

Beyond Reality: Evidence of Parallel Universes: My first book on the multiverse has far-out case histories you may enjoy reading. You'll find links to all my books on my main website by clicking on the Books tab: https://pastlifelady.com.

Coast to Coast AM: For tons of fun interviews on Akashic Records and more, I highly recommend *Coast to Coast AM*. Become a Coast Insider and listen to George Noory interview thousands of top professionals in this field and other paranormal realms.

Edgar Cayce: For more details on the life of the world's greatest psychic, Edgar Cayce, visit https://edgarcayce.org.

Healing Arts School: Check out my online school for classes in the Akashic Records and other fun topics including past-life regression, energy healing and more: https://healingarts.thinkific.com.

Dr. Linda Howe: For information on the Center for Akashic Studies and the wonderful work of Dr. Howe, visit https://lindahowe.com.

Jonathan and Andi Goldman: Sound pioneers with awesome healing music that will shift your frequencies: https://healingsounds.com.

Dr. Raymond Moody: Official website for Near Death Experiences pioneer Dr. Raymond Moody has a ton of amazing resources about the afterlife and more: https://lifeafterlife.com.

Stephen Halpern: One of my all-time favorites! Amazing music for body, mind, and spirit: https://www.stevenhalpernmusic.com.

Theosophical Society: The organization founded by Madame Blavatsky and others has resources and information about her work in the Akashic Records and other interesting subjects that formed the foundation of the New Age spiritual movement: https://www.theosophical.org/.

YouTube: Check out the videos on binaural beats and other relaxation music that you may enjoy.

TO WRITE TO THE AUTHOR

If you wish to contact the author or would like more information about this book, please write to the author in care of Llewellyn Worldwide Ltd. and we will forward your request. Both the author and publisher appreciate hearing from you and learning of your enjoyment of this book and how it has helped you. Llewellyn Worldwide Ltd. cannot guarantee that every letter written to the author can be answered, but all will be forwarded. Please write to:

Shelley A. Kaehr PhD
℅ Llewellyn Worldwide
2143 Wooddale Drive
Woodbury, MN 55125-2989

Please enclose a self-addressed stamped envelope for reply,
or $1.00 to cover costs. If outside the U.S.A., enclose
an international postal reply coupon.

Many of Llewellyn's authors have websites with additional information and resources. For more information, please visit our website at http://www.llewellyn.com.